MW00471634

Miracles
With A Message

Amazing true accounts and
the biblical lessons they teach.

Troy A. Brewer

PUBLISHED IN THE UNITED STATES OF AMERICA
BY
AVENTINE PRESS
San Diego, California
October, 2002
First Edition

To Leanna.

I thank God for the miracle of our marriage.

━━━━━━━━━━━

"One can either approach the world like
everything is a miracle
or nothing is a miracle.
I find the universe to be a miraculous place."
Albert Einstein

━━━━━━━━━━━

Thank you to Melanie Guinn for your hard work in helping me prepare this book. You are a blessing, Cousin!

Contents

Introduction

Living in the days of miracles

These are the days. If you ask a hundred different people to define the days we are living in, you might get a hundred different descriptions. Those in the work force and those trying to get back in the work force, would describe these as fiercely competitive days. Those that have loved ones in the armed forces would describe these as troubling days. The man or woman that respects the word of God would call these the last days. However you define the days we are living in, I think it's fair to say that all of us would agree that these are very busy days. To define our day as busy is really an understatement. A recent movie title would make a great heading for the page that describes these busy days.

"The Fast and the Furious"

Does it seem like days go by faster than they used to? Does it seem like the weeks and months just fly by? If you answered yes, first I want to tell you that yes, you are getting older. Besides that, I want to give you the reason for these fast and furious times. It all has to do with the busyness of our day.

I am writing this from my prayer room at my house here in Johnson County, Texas. I have lived here all my life and I've seen this part of the world change from a rural farmland to a suburb of the Dallas/Ft Worth Metroplex. It's incredible to consider the different world that I live in now, from the world that people lived in just 50 years ago in this same place.

A man in Johnson County just 50 years ago went to town only a few times a month. He was influenced by and had influence on only a handful of people because that was all he knew. He was isolated from the rest of the world around him. His worries, his hopes, and his griefs were restricted to what was going on in his immediate area. This was also true for all the generations before him.

Times Have Changed

Consider this. You are aware of more murders and deaths in one week than he was aware of his entire lifetime. You are aware and interact with more lives in one month that he might have in his entire lifetime. You are involved with more situations in one week than he was probably involved in his entire life. You travel more miles than he ever could in his entire lifetime. You see more, do more, interact with more and are involved with more people, places and things than any of our generations before us could imagine. We live more of a life in a year than those before us lived in an entire lifetime and that is something unique to our generation. It's not just you. It's not just me. It's all of us. Busyness is everywhere we look. It's in front of us. It's behind us. It's all around us. Everyday life is hard to keep up with.

Consider that every single day in the good 'ol USA: 10,813 people are born, 6,384 people die, 6,128 people get married, 2,688 couples file for divorce, 108,821 people go through hospital emergency rooms and that's just in one single day!

You know what? Even if you just sat there and did nothing, you would be busy. In a 24 hour period, if you're an adult of average weight:

Your heart beats 103,689 times
Your blood travels 168,000 miles
You breathe 23,040 times
You inhale 438 cubic feet of air.
You eat 3.25 pounds of food
You drink 2.9 quarts of liquids
You speak 4,800 words, including some unnecessary ones
You move 750 muscles
Your nails grow .000046 inch
Your hair grows .01714 inch
You exercise 7,000,000 brain cells.

No wonder you're worn out! Now with all of that going on every single day, it's easy to miss the advantage of the days we are living in. Like a car speeding past a historical marker, it's easy to pass important places and events because we are so busy getting somewhere or doing something. If we are not careful, all of our busyness will keep us oblivious to the special days that the Lord gives us and we will miss incredible opportunities that we cannot afford to lose. Eph. 5:15-16 says:

See then that ye walk circumspectly, not as fools,
but as wise,
redeeming the time, because the days are evil.

If you want to redeem or "cash in" on the day that you are living in, you've got to walk circumspectly, that is; know what's going on around you!

In every generation, in every lifetime, in every point in history, there are certain windows of opportunity where the timing is perfect for your life to be changed, for you to make a maximum impact on the world around you and for God to get maximum glory. Those certain windows of opportunity happen at certain times and if you don't know the day you are living in, you will miss the blessing that God has prepared for you!   I am here to tell you that even though most people don't know it, these are days that God is moving like never ever before. I am here to tell you that these are DAYS OF MIRACLES.

Bethlehem: The City that Missed Its Miracle

If God did an awesome miracle, I'm talking about the kind of miracle that would change your life or even change the world around you, do you think that you would know it? Not if you're too busy.

Case in point is the city of Bethlehem. Archeologists tell us that the well which supported the city of Bethlehem at the time of Jesus' birth could support a population of no more than 600. This has been a good rule of thumb to find the population numbers of ancient cities. Find the well that was contemporary to that generation and wha-lah, you have a pretty good estimation of the number of people living there at the time. The little town of Bethlehem had only several hundred people living there two-thousand years ago. Imagine the shock that Joseph must have felt returning there, when he topped that last hill with his young bride Mary and looked down on the town he knew from his childhood. Instead of finding a small town of "Mayberry", he looked down to what must of looked like Mardi gras!

Though the town could only support a few hundred people, there were thousands and thousands there because of the Roman decree commanding them to report to their place of birth for a census and taxation. That meant that everybody had to take their wealth with them. If your wealth was 300 sheep or 100 goats, not only were you looking for a place to stay in Bethlehem, but you were also looking for a place for your animals to stay.

What a mess! People and animals were everywhere. No one wanted to be there. Everything went slower than it should have had. The Roman soldiers hated every minute of it and took out their frustrations on whoever happened to be closest. Too many people crammed into too small a place, for too long of a time. Thousands of people were there.

So where are these people in scripture? If all of that is true, then how come we only see a handful of people privy to the miracle birth of Jesus Christ? Where are the other thousands that were in the same city? I will tell you where. They were there and they were clueless to the miracle. They were walking right past and living side-by-side to the greatest miracle the world had ever seen. The reason they missed the miracles going on around them was not because they hated God or were really bad people. They missed the miracles because they were busy! You never read about those thousands of people because they were busy being married, busy getting divorced, busy with their own births and busy with their own deaths. They were too caught up in the day-to-day busyness of life to be able to see that they were living in a special day of miracles.

Right now, in one day, more things happen to more people than what used to happen in an entire generation. Right now there are people in a running battle for their lives, while in another country there are people kicked back on the sofa with a remote in their hand. These are extreme days full of extreme people. What used to take a year can take a mere moment. What used to take a lifetime can be done twice within a year. People are busy, not realizing that these are no ordinary days. These are the last days and they are days of miracles.

The Case for Miracles

This little book is written as a testimony to the reality that Jesus Christ is alive and well and that His power is real in these extreme days. As real today as it was two-thousand years ago when He moved the stone and unwrapped the napkin that was tied around His face. These extreme days require an extreme move of the Lord. It's a perfect time for miracles.

Now, I have to tell you that for every amazing miracle you're going to read about in this book, I have seen thousands of hum-drum turnouts. For every one time I have seen God miraculously intervene, I have seen thousands of times when things turned out the way they were moving, even when it was really bad. Sometimes we see miracles and sometimes we don't, but God's power is just as real. I'm here to tell you that miracles are real.

"It is not just a provocative rumor that God has acted in His history, but a fact worthy of our intellectual conviction. The miracles of Christianity are not an embarrassment to the Christian worldview. Rather, they are testimony to the compassion of God for human beings benighted by sin and circumstance."

Gary Habermas, Christian & Scholar from his book "In Defense of Miracles" Co-written by R. Douglass Geivett. Intervarsity Press, 1997

"I like miracles because they cause the devil to run off screaming, 'no fair!'"

Troy Brewer, Pastor of Open Door Ministries, Joshua Texas.

If you were to stop by our little church, you would find a whole room full of changed lives that testify to the power of God. Some of them delivered from terrible things miraculously and some of them delivered through traditional or standard means. The proof in the pudding is that they are delivered and every one of them will give Jesus credit for it. The conclusion I come to is this; miracles are real because the intervening love of God is real.

Show Me the Power!

God has never been afraid to do miracles, nor has He ever been ashamed of the miracles He has done. Strangely, there has always been a big part of God's people who want to apologize for anything miraculous.

They tend to throw any modern day miracle into a re-volting blend of hillbilly folklore mixed well with a Roman stigmata. They do this because miracles tend to appeal to the emotion more than the intellect and that is offensive to some. These same people tend to believe that God is in the business of college education.

On the other hand, I understand how people can get to the point where they avoid the discussion of miracles. I have seen the mess about gold flakes and bleeding statues. I've seen the shows on public television where they exploit the services of Pentecostal snake handlers. I have had my cringe meter pegged more than once by a late night evangelist selling "miracle water". But in the midst of all the stupidity that seeps out from our church buildings and into the light of the general public, there is no excuse for the people of God to not believe that God is who He says He is. Miracles are real because God is who He advertises. We need not fear that the love of God is not genuine.

A few years ago, a movie came out with a line that became part of our pop culture, "Show me the money!" This little slogan soon became the battle cry for a skeptical generation. Just like that, our generation looks at the church, saying to themselves that they have heard the hype, now show me the power! If you say you have love, show me. If you say you have peace, show me. If you say you have the answer, then show me. Show me the power! There is nothing worse than something that is not what it advertises. It makes people regret that they trusted whatever it is they bought into. To be as subtle as a meat cleaver, it makes God want to lose His lunch.

A Lesson in Advertising

Laodicia was a town in the Roman Empire that happened to be the very first city in the world to boast of hot and cold running water. They used the Roman technology of aqueducts to transport hot water from hot springs several miles away from the city. They also moved in cold water from cold springs several miles from the other direction. It was an amazing vision and only Rome had the confidence and the money to pull off such a venture. The prospect of having hot and cold water caused people from all over the empire to flock to Laodicia. This was just one more proof that Roman genius and ingenuity could make life better in every way.

There was a problem with the system though. The technology to transport water through insulated pipes was more than a thousand years away. In those days the water bridges were "open-air" in design and by the time the hot water got to its destination, it was no longer hot. By the time the cold water got there it was no longer cold. Like the fabled king that was naked (the Emperor's new clothes), nobody dared to say anything about Roman design being a failure. They drank the nasty water and boasted to the world that they had it better than everybody else. The day the project was completely finished, a Roman authority came to be a part of what we would call, the ribbon-cutting ceremony. There was pomp and pageant, music, food, laughter. Then everyone got quiet as the dignitary took his famous first drink from the fountain that advertised it was cold. To the embarrassment of all the city officials standing there, he spit it out and said it was disgusting! The word went out quickly through Rome that the water was not as advertised, but that it was plain old "luke or light warm".

You can then imagine the impact Jesus made on the church in that area when He declared the following word found in Revelation 3:14-17

"And to the angel of the church of the Laodiceans write, 'These things say the Amen, the Faithful and True Witness, the Beginning of the creation of God: "I know your works, that you are neither cold nor hot. I could wish you were cold or hot. So then, because you are lukewarm, and neither cold nor hot, I will vomit you out of my mouth. Because you say, 'I am rich, have become wealthy, and have need of nothing'--and do not know that you are wretched, miserable, poor, blind, and naked."
NKJV

They understood the message. It was something that really hit home. They were not what they advertised and it made God sick. They were a church that promised more of everything, but actually had less than most. When inspection day came, they were shamed.

I'm here to tell you that inspection day is coming and you better have power. It's a terrible thing for us as Christians to say we have something if we don't really have it.

Without a display of changed lives, our boastings are actually false advertisement. We say that Jesus saves. We say that Jesus heals. We say that Jesus Christ is able to turn bitter places sweet and dark places light. We say that God is willing to step into your life and clean you and set you free. We say that our God is not passively sitting by waiting for you to die, but that He actively longs to be involved in every part of your life, if your willing to humble yourself and let him be God. If we say that, we should be able to produce a line of people, places and events where God is doing just that.

James, the half-brother of Jesus threw a wrench into a lot of people's theology when he wrote the radical line that would become scripture.

> *"...Faith by itself, if it does not have works, is dead. But someone will say, "You have faith, and I have works." Show me your faith without your works, and I will show you my faith by my works."*
> *James 2:17-19 NKJV*

In other words, faith is not a theory. Faith is something that will produce something else. While faith starts out invisible, it does not remain that way. James says, I will show you my faith.

This book is one small attempt to show you my faith. My faith being that Jesus loves you and will change your life if you let Him.

What gets the attention of people today is not great sermons or nice buildings. Every cause you can imagine has a great speaker and a home office, but only the Church has the power of Jesus. It is just so important for people to know that Jesus is the God that sees and moves on behalf of His people. His power to save is understood through His power to heal, clean, protect, prosper and make things right.

Looking for Power in All the Wrong Places

People flock by the millions and pack out movie houses to view stories like the X-men, Spiderman, Harry Potter, Star Wars and Lord of the Rings because these movies portray people that have a leg up on everybody else around them. They have "power". That's what people wish they had.

How tragic it is that there is a church on every corner here in the states, but the USA doesn't know where the power is. It is so important for the church to declare that God is a miracle working God. Not just for the time that great men of God put pen to paper, inspired by the Holy Spirit, but for this time as well. He is not less of a God now than what He used to be, nor is He less of a God now than what He someday will be. He is God right now! Right this very minute.

Let's throw away the doctrine that says God will be powerful again someday. Let's throw it on the scrap heap of ideas we have held onto, while the world around us has gone to hell. Let's throw that bit of dogma right on top of the belief that God only used to be powerful. I think there are a lot of people that don't believe in the power of God for today, because they don't want to be held responsible for walking in the power of God today. They want to be called righteous, but they never see God move. Lord help us! If that's you, let me be the first one to invite you to go into plumbing, or some kind of computer work, but get out of the business of preaching the Gospel because you muddy up the water for the rest of us.

Because of these kinds of teachings, the power of God has to be taught to the average Joe in the church today.

More importantly, the average Joe that's lost needs to be *shown* the power of God today. It's our duty as drop-dead-sold-out-Jesus-freaks to prove and teach the power of God. This is not a new phenomenon. It was something that had to be shown and taught in Jesus' day as well.

Setting Martha Strait

Consider carefully how Jesus set Martha strait when He begin to make it real to her that Lazarus would not be dead for very much longer (John 11:20-27). Yes, Lazarus had assumed room temperature, but Life had just shown up. Now the problem was that Martha thought she was supposed to wait on some dispensation or special day in order for her to get her miracle. No doubt she had been taught that (from someone I would have encouraged to get a different kind of job). So Jesus let her in on what was going to happen by simply saying, " Your brother will rise again".

> *Martha then said to Him, "I know that He will rise again in the resurrection at the last day." Jesus said to her, "I am the resurrection and the life. He who believes in Me, though he may die, he shall live. And whoever lives and believes in Me shall never die. Do you believe this?" She said to Him, "Yes, Lord, I believe that You are the Christ, the Son of God, who is to come into the world."*
> *John 11:24-27 NKJV*

She basically said, "I believe that you're going to be powerful someday," but Jesus changed her doctrine by revealing to her that He was powerful right now. He then asked her the question, "Do you believe this?"

The Holy Spirit did a work in her as she looked into His incredible Jewish eyes. A revelation landed right in the midst of her heart. "Yes" she said as the light came on, "I believe that you are the Christ, the son of the living God, who is come into the world." Notice the present tense in what she is saying. " You *are* the Christ" not "you *were* the Christ" or "you *are going to be* the Christ". She didn't say, you *did come* into the world or you *will come* into the world, she said you *are* the son of the living God who *is* come into the world. Jesus made her understand that His power is present tense. My great desire is that the church would get that revelation.

Turn the Light On!

There is a balance that needs to be taught concerning the working of miracles. Just because God does a miracle is not His stamp of approval on somebody's life. Nor is the lack of a miracle God's stamp of disapproval. God's mercy is revealed in lots of different ways, miracles being only one of those ways. We will get to that balance later in this book. Until then, what you will find is a collection of what I would define as real life miracles that I have personally seen happen over the past few years of having an eye to see and an ear to hear. Some of them may seem much more miraculous than others, but they were all instances where God stepped in and changed things for a different outcome; an outcome where He gets glorified and hopefully you get encouraged.

Read these stories and let your heart rejoice. If God can do these incredible things for my friends and me, He can do them for you. We sure don't have the market cornered when it comes to seeing God move. I am telling you, one of the most wonderful characteristics of miracles is that they are always personal. The love that God has for you, my friend, is a very personal love. I have seen Him demonstrate it over and over again to people that I have pastored and people that I have been blessed to be hooked up with in some way.

Don't let anybody tell you differently.

These are the days.

Chapter

1

A Money Miracle

There is no way I could list the miracles I've seen without having at least one "money miracle" in it. I am no Donald Trump, so the Lord has had to bail me out of some big financial messes in different times of my life and ministry. Out of all those times, there is one financial breakthrough that really stands out in my mind as a miracle.

The Early & Vulnerable Days

1995 was a year of miracles. It had to be because of the mess we were in. As I have already stated, miracles are not God's best for His people. Miracles are there for God's people when a miracle is required. The fertile ground that bears the fruit of a miraculous move of God is typically a dangerous place to stand. You don't see God doing miracles of provision when there is money in the bank and a 7-11 on the corner. You don't hear of the miracle healing of a skin disorder, when all you have to do is apply a cream that your insurance will pay for. No, miracles are powerful moves for very desperate times. That's an important biblical principle to learn.

Some of the most mind-bending manifestations of God are born in the midst of chaos and controversy. It was like that when God made a way through the Red Sea for the children of Israel. It was that way when Jesus was born in Bethlehem. It's that way for some of you reading this. Against all odds, the hand of God moves. While all the world sees is the pain and conflict, you finally see your miracle that others pass by.

That's how I would sum up my first year of ministry, "powerful moves of God in very desperate times". So when I say that 1995 was a year of miracles, you understand that it was a dangerous time for Leanna and I. Not because our lives were in peril, but because we were in the infant stages of something from the Lord and so much was on the line. I want to stop right here and remind you that this is always the devil's plan. To destroy a work of God before it's able to stand and fight a good fight. Rev 12:4 says:

> **"...and the dragon stood before the woman who was ready to give birth, to devour her Child as soon as it was born."**

The cosmic punk, who the world knows as the devil, is not a brilliant strategist. He is merely a relentless opportunist. He is not a general, he is only a bully. He is not looking for just anything to devour, but according to 1 Peter 5:8 he is going about as a roaring lion seeking *whom he may* devour; those he has permission to devour. Those that do not know any better, who give place or open a door for him to tear them to pieces. That's why the first part of the verse says be sober and be vigilant. There's a bully on your block and if you give him the chance, he will be happy to clean your clock! Pardon me for being the preacher right here, but listen to the warning that God gave Cain thousands of years ago.

Then the Lord said to Cain, "Why are you angry? And why has your countenance fallen? "If you do well, will not your countenance be lifted up? And if you do not do well, sin is crouching at the door; and its desire is for you, but you must master it."
Genesis 4:6 and 7 NASB

It's been the same way for 6,000 years. There is a devil at the door for every one of us and if we don't do right, guess who's coming for dinner? It's a good day to take things seriously.

So understand this, infants don't know any better and they tend to do things not knowing how dangerous those things are. The devil knows how that works and that's why he is there in the infant stages of your walk with God. You finally start going to church and some dummy makes you so mad you consider not going back. He is there in the infant stages of your marriage, your parenting, your college education, your career and yes, even your ministry. Right now might be a great time for you to stop and ask God to help you to "MASTER" the devil at your door.

A Bible Thump'n Repo-man.

So let me set up the story about the miracle. You know how the beginning of Oliver Twist starts out? "It was the best of times and the worst of times." That's a

great way to describe our first year of ministry. To tell
you the truth, that's a great way to describe our
ministry today. Right now we are involved in so many
hurting lives and fighting bigger battles than I ever
imagined, but at the same time we are seeing God do
things that others only dream about. If there is
anything I have learned about God, it is that He can't
stand to be bored. I like that about God.

The years before our ministry, I had worked my way
into management at the home office of a large insurance company. God had granted me favor and after
several years, the money finally started to be there.
Just about the time things really started looking up, a
bigger fish of another company swallowed up our big
fish of a company and all of us were beating the
pavement for a new job.

After a little while, I found myself employed by a national rent-to-own outfit. Before long, I was a glorified
repo-man. The money was good and the opportunity
for ministry was even better. It was through this job
that people in the projects surrounding Ft. Worth,
Texas began to trust me. It was through this job that
God took me into the homes of the poorest of Ft.
Worth's poor and showed me first hand what a difference mercy and compassion made in the lives of
really poor people. I didn't realize it at the time, but I
was in seminary, in training and being prepared to be a
pastor.

Imagine what this was like. I would knock on a door at
7:00 a.m. and a sleepy-eyed single mom would open
the door. "Mrs. Jones", I would say, " I'm here to pick
up our refrigerator."   She would look at me in disgust

and explain that there was milk for her kids in the refrigerator and meat in the freezer for supper. Then I
would explain that she
had broken her contract and failed to report her last
move to us and that it had taken me several weeks to
track her down. I would be polite, even sympathetic,
but I would be firm. "I am here to take the refrigerator". I would say. I can't tell you how hard it was
to wheel past those kids without saying anything. The
absolute worst thing I could have said at that point was
something like "God bless you", or "Jesus loves you."
It was important at that moment to just keep my mouth
shut and do my job professionally.

Now imagine how effective it was to show up at that
same house later when I was off of work with a used,
but very good, refrigerator that Leanna and I had
bought from a second hand store. Imagine the surprise
on that momma's face when I explained to her that
earlier I had been there in the name of my company,
but this time I was there in the name of Jesus. The refrigerator was a free gift, "just like Jesus", I would say.
Then you can believe that a move of God would
follow.

Those were special times for us. At the same time this
was going on, we began to do our first feeding outreaches in different parts of town as a way to gain
influence in peoples lives. Leanna and I sowed a lot
into the lives of poor people those 2 years, not knowing
that we would be poorer than them for our first 3 or 4
years of ministry.

The Money Miracle

When we stepped out in faith to start our ministry, we really stepped out. No income. No net to fall back on, just an absolute affirmation that this was what God wanted us to do.

Man did we get busy! My good friend Mark Berry, of Bread Basket Ministries, really helped us out with food to give away and prisons to preach in. I don't really know what we would have done without his financial and spiritual help.

We started having church meetings on Sunday at Leanna's mother's daycare building. While we began to see lives changed and souls saved, I soon found out that feeding poor people and preaching in prisons does not pay the bills. We had four little kids including a set of twins that were three, and I mean times got hard.

The cable man turned off the hell-a-vision. I began to know our bill collectors by first name, that is until my phone got disconnected. When our electricity got turned off, I remember lots of candlelight dinners. Our son Benjamin, who was about 5 at the time, thinking the whole time that we were playing a game called "olden days". I also remember Leanna's confident voice and soothing words as she assured me that things would not always be like this. She was amazing.

We agreed to just do all we could do to pay the house payment and let everything else go. We didn't want to loose the house. We didn't want to loose anything, but the house was a special gift from the Lord and we were believing that God was going to let us hang on to it somehow.

In our first year of ministry our combined household income was just over $7,000.00. The only payment we made was the house payment and after a while we couldn't even make that.

During the day I would see people saved and set free. At one point I was preaching in seventeen prisons a month and doing three weekly food outreaches. But at nighttime I would come home to a house that was three months past due on the mortgage with no electricity. It really was the best of times and the worst of times all at the same time. Sometimes that's the walk.

The day the man from the mortgage company came was a day I will never forget. I spied on him through the blinds as he walked around my house with a pad in his hand. I plotted his death and burial as others had plotted mine just a year before. I remember little Ben following him around, amused that somebody had come to visit us. I remember praying a simple "please help us, Jesus" prayer as he came to the door. When he began speaking, I already knew the drill. He politely, but firmly, explained that we had broken our contract and he was there for the house. I asked him to give me a bottom dollar amount and last due date to get it paid. After some figuring he said, "Unless you have a check for just over $1,700 at the mortgage company in Memphis Tennessee by 5:00 pm next Friday, you will have 30 days to vacate the premises." There was no more grace period. Everything was way past due.

He saw that the electricity was off and then I saw him glance at my kids. I recognized a familiar feeling behind his eyes. He didn't like that we all saw him as the bad guy. So at that point I assured him that we didn't think he was the bad guy. I began to talk to him about Jesus. Can you imagine the irony of me consoling the man that was there to repo my house? I was well trained to do that in seminary.

I had poured my whole life into being a blessing to others, but couldn't find a way to bless my own family with a way to keep the house. It was, as I said, a dangerous hour for us. Would I throw my hands in the air and decide that I had given it my best shot? I have to tell you the answer to that question was yes. That is, if it were not for Leanna. "Don't you curse our house by giving up on God", she would say. I already told you, she was amazing. So onward I would go, encouraged just enough to keep going.

The weekend came and went without anything really happening. We turned over the couch and dug through the car ashtrays and found enough change to give the very last dime we had to somebody we were feeding. I know that sounds crazy, but we were planting a seed because that was all we could do. I mean we were already broke, so what difference did a couple of more dollars make? My emotions were a real roller coaster, but sometimes I would really believe that I should expect Jesus to show up on my doorsteps the way we had showed up at so many others' doorsteps.

Monday came and went. Nothing. Tuesday came. Still nothing. Wednesday came and I happened to be outside when the mailman showed up. I thought I would save Leanna the grief by going through today's pile of bad news. In the midst of the stack of over due bills, I came across an envelope that caused what little sanity I had left to run for it's life. To my horror, I read the return name and address and it said "INTERNAL REVENUE SERVICE". "That's great!", I thought, "Now I am being audited!" I opened up the envelope and started reading the letter. After a little jargon, I came to the point where it explained that several years ago we had paid too much money on our taxes and that the IRS was voluntarily sending me a check for that amount.

Did you understand what I just said? The I.R.S. was voluntarily sending me money they owed me without me knowing they owed it to me! Now if that does not define MIRACLE to you, call your doctor!

In that same batch of mail was another envelope with a check for just over $1,700.00. The amount of money we so desperately needed. Jesus had showed up on my doorstep. The next day we FedEx'd that check to the mortgage company, which they received at 1:11 pm on Friday. We have never missed a house payment since.

The Message in the Miracle

If you need a miracle of provision in your life, let me encourage you. Jesus still shows up at doorsteps. He still makes house calls. He goes door-to-door even to this day asking to be let in. Rev 3:20 says:

> *"Behold, I stand at the door and knock.*
> *If anyone hears My voice*
> *and opens the door, I will come in to him and dine*
> *with him, and he with Me."*
> *NKJV*

When He says He will come in and eat with us, Jesus gives us the picture of family; a bunch of people sitting and eating together like a scene from the "Walton's". Pay close attention to this too. Jesus doesn't knock with his hand, He knocks with his voice. Many times we are looking for the hand of God instead of listening for the voice of God. As I have stated in this story, there are times when you need the hand of God as I have many times, but make sure you don't miss His voice while in search for His hand. As wonderful as miracles are, we don't live by them. We live by faith and faith comes from "hearing", the Bible says.

Your miracle is coming, but you don't want to look for your miracle at the expense of missing the Master. Make sure that if you're looking for a free gift from God, that you don't miss His greatest gift, Jesus. Because Jesus truly is the gift that keeps on giving!

> *For God so loved the world that He gave His only*
> *begotten Son, that whoever*
> *believes in Him should not perish,*
> *but have everlasting life.*
> *John 3:16 NKJV*

The saying that you can't out give God is truer than you think. God is the greatest of all givers.

Chapter
2

Miracle on a
Hot Tin Roof

Miracle Beginnings

It all started with an 80 year-old man trying to re-shingle his elderly neighbor's roof all by himself. He had seen the need of this widow woman and decided that he was going to do something about it. One shingle at a time...one day at a time. See, he figured about all the strength he had was to carry one shingle up the ladder, nail it down and climb back down again, before the Texas heat put him under. So that's what he did. One shingle every day. On the day my father-in-law drove by his house, the old man was resting before climbing down again.

Ray Knight, my father-in-law, is the kind of guy that probably doesn't like you unless you're the underdog somehow. If he does like you, he would do anything and I mean anything for you. The funny thing about Ray is, he doesn't have to know you to like you and he doesn't care if you like him. He looked up, saw the old man and decided he liked him. A moment later he was on the roof, introducing himself as a roofer who wanted to help.

That night he called me with a high suggestion that I come and help that next day. I had just married his daughter and still felt the need to impress him in those days, so I agreed. When I hung up the phone that night, I had no idea that I was entering into a ministry and this was the beginning of a lifetime call to servitude. Even though I was already saved and living for Jesus, God was about to wake me up out of a lifetime coma.

I met the old man and we re-roofed the old woman's house. By the end of the week we knew that these old folks could use some help in groceries, so we brought some on Saturday. They suggested we visit their elderly friend across the street with groceries and those people suggested we visit someone they knew. By the end of the month I was spending my Saturdays taking food and friendship to the elderly of Samson Park, Texas. By the end of that first summer, we had more than 50 houses we were visiting and before I knew it, I had a full-blown ministry on my hands.

The whole door-to-door thing is why we first called our ministry "Open Door". All that we do now was birthed out of the miracles we saw in those first 2 years of being committed to old people that others didn't care about. Since this ministry was born on a rooftop it is only fitting that we would see an incredible miracle concerning a roof.

A Twenty-Year Problem

Bread Basket Ministries of Ft. Worth supplied enough groceries for us every Saturday and off we would go. I employed my kids in on this and would get a big kick out of watching the old folks nearly hug them to death. One lady in particular would always come to the gate and just let me hand her the food over her little chain link fence.

There was something there I couldn't quite put my finger on. I could tell that she was uneasy about us coming into her home. I'm a big ugly guy and at first I just thought it was me, but after a while it became apparent that it was something else. With me being as subtle as a meat cleaver, I finally just asked what the problem was. She blushed a little and said that she was too embarrassed to have people in her home. Her roof had leaked badly for more than 20 years and had caused her wooden floors to rot as well.

I couldn't wait for her to finish her sentence before I could offer to round up the guys to fix that problem. I knew better than to do that though. Now in my mind, I already had a plan to try and raise the money for the materials and gather the men to do the job. I wanted to be careful however not to promise something that I couldn't deliver quickly and correctly. I did not want to loose the Godly influence I had in this sweet lady's life. So, I asked her if she would pray with me for God to do a miracle concerning the roof of her house. She said she would feel silly asking God to roof her house when so many other people needed things. She was a really sweet lady, but that mentality had kept her from being blessed for a really long time. I told her to get over her feelings and grab a hold of GOD! And before she could interject, my kids and I had hold of her hand and were praying for a miracle.

That week I made some arrangements with several people about helping me roof her house. When

Saturday came, as I was delivering her food, I had planned on telling her that her new roof was in the works. I never got to tell her though.

New Roof, New House, and a New Level of Faith

When I pulled up to that house the next week, it was a brand new house! New roof included! New paint job, a whole new house!

As I was saying to the kids, "Hey guys look at this", she came running out to the gate. I had never seen her so excited and full of life. See, we had prayed for God to give her a new roof on Saturday. On Tuesday, the city was putting up a new telephone poll next to her house and it crashed right through her roof! It was an election year and nobody wanted any bad press about making a sweet old lady homeless, so by Friday she had a new roof, new frame work and a brand new paint job, all at the expense of the city. On Saturday, I went into her house for the first time and we blessed the house with prayer. What an awesome and quick turn around!

The Message in the Miracle

When I look back on that miracle, it seems to me that God had been waiting for years to give that woman a new roof. Sadly though, it had never occurred to her to ask God to meet that need. "It was too trivial", she must of thought. "My life is just not that important to the Lord." She was wrong on both counts. Her life was important to the Lord and yes, He did want her house to be fixed and not rotting and shameful. But the deal was, she had to ask and she had to ask on His terms.

Listen very careful to what Jesus says in Matthew 7:7-12:

"Ask, and it will be given to you; seek, and you will find; knock, and it will be opened to you. For everyone who asks receives, and he who seeks finds, and to him who knocks it will be opened. Or what man is there among you who, if his son asks for bread, will give him a stone? Or if he asks for a fish, will He give him a serpent? If you then, being evil, know how to give good gifts to your children, how much more will your Father who is in heaven give good things to those who ask Him! Therefore, whatever you want men to do to you, do also to them, for this is the Law and the Prophets. NKJV

I want to encourage you as Jesus encourages you. Ask!!! Humble your heart and let God get involved in your life. He may have a miracle a few days away that you have been waiting on for years.

Chapter

3

Flight 191

August 2, 1985 is a day I will never forget. It was prime time for me. I had just graduated high school in May, I was eighteen, and in my mind completely "bullet-proof". Besides playing music in a band here and there, I had a good job and was really starting to stretch my wings. This was a day I didn't have to work, so I spent the afternoon with my dad at his house. Dad and I were watching a videotape flick. Remember this was 1985, when VCR's were a big deal.

At the same time I balled-up on the couch to watch the tube, 1,500 miles away a Delta Airlines flight 191, a Lockheed L-1011, lifted off from runway 9L at the Fort Lauderdale/Hollywood International Airport. It took off without any problems and veered into a clear blue sky. Aboard that aircraft were 167 passengers and crew that were traveling to Los Angeles with a stop at Dallas/Ft. Worth. I didn't know it then, but by the end of this day, I wouldn't feel nearly as "bullet-proof", because a life-changing event would fly right into my family. On board this aircraft were not just 167 people, but a miracle that I am writing about seventeen years later.

An Invisible Enemy in the Air

For the people on board that day, this was a routine flight. The passengers were served, people were reading magazines, but as the flight cruised over the farmlands and swamps of Louisiana, something strange began to happen at Dallas.

In command of Delta 191 was Captain Edward Conners, a 14,000-hour pilot who was highly respected at Delta. Assisting him on the flight deck was First Officer Rudolph Price, hardly a novice, and Second Officer Nick Nassick. Nassick actually re-wrote the technical manual for Delta's L-1011's some two years earlier and he probably knew the inner workings of the airplane more than anyone present. If there were ever a capable crew to fly a commercial jet, this was it. The strange thing that was happening in Dallas, though, was something that no crew could tackle. It was something that would not fight fair.

As the plane approached the beginning of the standard terminal arrival route, Air Traffic Control gave the crew a vector to "turn heading 290....". Seeing a thunderstorm cell at that heading, and not being one to trifle with heavy weather, Captain Conners decided to turn to a heading of 255 and turn back to 290 before he got to Blue Ridge. This would give the passengers a much smoother ride, even if it cost the flight a few extra minutes. Meanwhile, off the end of runway 17L at DFW, a huge updraft had begun to form and a record-breaking thunderstorm was forming with more energy than 100 nuclear reactors. It didn't move in from far away, it formed in a moment, right at the end of the runway. All of this, however, was disguised in the form of puffy, white clouds and nobody knew it. Something invisible was lurking at the end of that runway; something that would bring a plane down. At the National Weather Office in Dallas, the aviation meteorologist decided to break for an early dinner, since nothing was on his scope that afternoon. He wasn't there to see or report the monster microburst that erupted that day. He would later return from dinner just in time to learn that an airliner crashed at DFW.

Turning onto final approach, flight 191 was at 2,000 feet AGL with the landing gear in motion. The landing checklist was performed without incident. Flight 191 was four miles behind a Learjet that was landing at the same runway, and throughout the entire ordeal, he never reported any abnormal weather phenomenon. Approaching 1,500 feet, F. O. Price commented, "There's lightning coming out of that one." Captain Conners, surprised, replied "What?" "There's lightning coming out of that one." "Where?" "Right ahead of us." That was the first sign of trouble in the cockpit of Flight 191.

Descending through 800 feet, something very odd began to happen. The plane began to speed up, without anyone touching the throttles. The landing speed for that airplane's weight was 149 knots, and all of the sudden the plane accelerated to 173 knots before Price (who was the pilot flying), closed the throttles to slow her down. Captain Conners recognized this as the first signs of wind shear, and warned Price: "Watch your speed. You're gonna lose it all of the sudden, there it is." No sooner had he said it, when the plane lost speed and Price advanced the throttles. "Push it up, push it way up. Way up, way up, way up," exclaimed Conners. From the beginning to the end of his sentence, the aircraft's speed dropped from 173 to 133 knots. As Price gave it full power, the passengers could feel the strange sensation of speeding up and then what must of felt like the slamming on of breaks. Captain Conners, his voice filled with terror, exclaimed, "Hang onto it!" as the speed dropped to 119. To avoid a stall, the pilots pushed the nose over... their vertical speed increased to 1,700 feet per minute and the ground proximity warning began to sound an alarm. Like an extreme ride at nearby Six Flags, everyone's stomachs must have jumped into their throats as the plane plunged near to the ground. The last words heard in the cockpit were various expletives.

As the plane flew into the microburst, a tremendous downdraft slammed 191 down several hundred feet at once. The aircraft landed in a field, bounced in the air, and came down again on Hwy 114. A small Honda driven by a Delta employee on his first week on the job was crushed by the number one engine, killing the driver, and shutting that engine down. The differential thrust with the failed engine caused the plane to veer left, and in one horrifying moment, it struck two 4 million gallon water tanks at a ground speed of 220 knots.

As horrified onlookers watched, flight 191 exploded with a mixture of water, metal and fire. Bodies and debris were scattered and thrown. On that terrible day at DFW, 167 passengers were driven literally into the ground by an invisible force that some would call an act of God. It was no act of God, but a diabolical series of events driven by the devil and cloaked in a natural phenomenon. There were a few survivors (which was the act of God), but 136 people faced eternity that day and thousands of people began to mourn their loss.

So where's the Miracle and what does this have to do with me? You might be wondering why I would include this story in the midst of my "victory list". The truth is, I wasn't anywhere near DFW that day, but nonetheless I have a strange connection to that flight. Every time I think about it, I see the hand of God moving on the behalf of my immediate family in a day when most of us didn't have a clue. 1985 was "B.C." for me. I wouldn't have an honest and submissive en-counter with Jesus until May the next year. My brothers and sisters and in-laws would all come to the Lord in the 90's and be what I would call, drop-dead-sold-out-Jesus Freaks. Let me tell you though, a lot of that nearly didn't happen because of Flight 191. You see, my little sister was supposed to be on that plane. And when you find out why she wasn't on board, you'll see why I call it a miracle!

Sifting Through the Wreckage

At a little after 5:00 that afternoon, I remember my Dad looking at his watch and saying, "Missy ought to be landing right about now." No sooner had he said that, than Brad Wright of Channel 5 News, stopped what he was reporting to say that they had just got word that a crash had happened at DFW Airport. That prompted a lot of phone calls and several hours of fear and des-peration. It's a terrible thing for anyone to have to go through. The reports were vague and unclear.

At first it was only known that it was a commercial airliner that had crashed around 5:15. Missy was supposed to land at about that time. Then it was re-ported that it was a Delta Flight. Missy's plane was a Delta plane. Then it was reported that it was a flight

from Ft. Lauderdale. That clinched it; Missy's flight
was from Ft. Lauderdale.

A family member named Mike, knew of Missy's
arrival. He worked at DFW airport, as did my dad.
When the crash happened, he was not far away and
within minutes he was sifting through the wreckage
looking for my sister. He looked into the bloody faces
of one body after another expecting to see the face of
Missy. It was something that I am not sure he ever re-
covered from. It no doubt had a powerful effect on
him, as it would anybody. But Missy's lifeless body
was not among that wreckage. He didn't know it.
Neither did we. In fact all of the family would be convinced that Missy had died until a little after 7:00 that
evening.

While Mike went through the wreckage and all of us
made frantic phone calls, Missy was west bound in
another aircraft trying to think of a way to undo a
terrible mess that had happened at customs. A mess
that caused her and the family she was traveling with to
miss their flight. A "mess" that was actually orches-
trated by God.

A Mess That Makes a Miracle

Missy was about to turn 14 when she got invited to go
to Bermuda by a girl she knew from school. The
parents of her friend were planning on a week full of
parties and they didn't want to bother with the inconve-
nience of being a parent, so the routine was that their
little girl would bring a friend. They didn't know it at
the time, but their lives depended on Missy going on
this trip.

The two little girls spent most of their week by themselves hanging out on the beach or swimming at the hotel. The night before they were to head back to Texas, the mom of Missy's friend got very upset with Missy. Alcohol had a lot to do with the woman's frame of mind, but for no apparent reason that Missy could see, the woman went off on a verbally violent tangent. She called Missy terrible names, as the rest of the family went about business as usual. That night she made Missy pack her bag and get it ready for in the morning, when they would be leaving. She made sure her birth certificate was right on top so that she would not have to dig for it the next day at the airport.

The next morning they all got up early and double-checked everything. Again everybody made sure Missy had her birth certificate right on top of all of her clothes because she was the only one that did not have a passport. Missy had seen her friend's mom's violent rages and she didn't want to do anything to make her angry again.

After a 12-seat puddle jumper trip across to Ft. Lauderdale, everybody got off the plane and quickly went through customs. Since Missy's birth certificate was in her suitcase, she had to wait until the baggage was unloaded. The mom and dad, not ones to be inconvenienced, decided to let Missy fend for herself and they went through customs without her. When her suitcase was finally handed to her, she opened it up and to her horror she discovered her birth certificate was not there. How could that be? She had double-checked it back at Bermuda and this was exactly what she didn't want to happen. Missy began to frantically tear through all of her clothes looking for the white piece of paper.

On the other side of a chain-link fence stood the family, tapping their feet and looking at their watches. Everyone was afraid that mom was about to explode again. It didn't take long before she began to go into one of her rages. When she saw Missy looking through her bags, she began to yell and curse across the way. Poor Missy's internal cringe meter began to peg as the realization hit her that the birth certificate was just not there. She wasn't about to tell her vulgar host what the problem was though.

Before long, a lady in customs began to help Missy go through her bags. She saw how ugly the woman was being, yelling at Missy, so she began to try to calm Missy's nerves and help fix the problem like a rational adult. She assured her that she was not stupid, as the lady was yelling, and that this kind of thing happened sometimes. After she went through Missy's bags, they both went to the officer's boss where they discussed what they were going to do. The person in authority told Missy and then her friend's parents

that they could not let her through customs without proper identification. Another copy would have to be sent from Texas and remember this was 3 to 4 years before anyone had a fax machine.

The mother began to go ballistic! She screamed, she yelled, she called everybody names. She threatened. She cursed. She made a real fool out of herself. Missy was glad at this point that she was on the other side of the fence. This outburst went on for fifteen or twenty minutes when Missy decided to look one more time in her suitcase, because she knew for a fact that she had put it in there with the rest of her clothes. As she walked over to her suitcase, which was still on a customs table and laid wide open, she could see a white piece of paper laying in it. She knew what it was before she even got there. There in plain view, but for some reason unseen by her and several customs agents, was her birth certificate! It was just lying there where everybody should have been able to see it.

Within a moment, Missy went through customs, and the entire family began running through the airport trying to catch their plane. For the entire sprint to their gate this woman continued to unleash her verbal septic tank on my sister. When they finally got to the gate, they were informed that the plane was finished boarding and that they had just missed it. " We haven't missed it!", the woman demanded. "It hasn't left yet, let us on board!" Just outside the window they could see the plane was still sitting at the gate. Maybe it was the woman's mouth, maybe it was that the clerk was in a bad mood, but for whatever reason, that Delta employee refused to let them on board and they watched as flight 191 backed up from the gate and preceded to take off. Two hours later, that same airplane would be fragmented into a million pieces.

The dad, who had no skill at helping a 13-year-old girl get through customs, apparently knew how to get another ticket and fifteen minutes later they were on board another airplane. One that would not crash into 8 million gallons of tanked water at the end of runway 17L. One that would get them home safely and not send that woman and her hen-pecked husband to hell that day. It was a miracle that they *were not* on board that plane.

Missy would grow up, get saved and for several years
work with her husband as a children's pastor before be-
coming a nurse. Literally thousands of lives would be
touched through her service and ministry that might not
have otherwise, if an angel had not blinded the eyes of
everybody in customs back in 1985. Now you know
why the crash of Delta 191 is on my victory list.

The Message in the Miracle

Be not hasty in thy spirit to be angry: for anger
resteth in the bosom of fools.
Eccl 7:9 KJV

I bet you think that when they all arrived in Texas, literally flying over the wreckage of the plane they
should have been on, the irate mom gave Missy a big
apology. I bet you think that when they found out what
had happened they were relieved and grateful, right?
That's what I would of thought, but I would have been
wrong. You see, the Bible calls ungodly people "brute
beasts" for good reason. Like animals, people without
the mind of Christ only deal with what they want, when
they want it. Natural man, when he is not thankful, has
his foolish heart darkened and doesn't even know he is
blessed. This was the case with the family that my
sister was tagging with that week. Look at what Missy
e-mailed me about what happened when they got back
and read it in her own words:

*"IT DIDN'T TAKE VERY LONG FOR US TO GET TO
FT. WORTH, BUT WHEN WE DID WE HAD TO
CIRCLE FOR A LONG TIME AND I COULD SEE
THE CRASH FROM MY SEAT BUT REALLY DIDN'T
KNOW IT WAS ALL THAT BAD. I COULD SEE THE*

FIRE TRUCKS AND SMOKE, BUT JUST DIDN'T THINK IT WAS A DISASTER LIKE IT WAS. THE PILOT DID TELL US THERE WAS AN ACCIDENT AND THAT WE HAD TO CIRCLE TO I THINK, COME IN ON A DIFFERENT RUN WAY BUT HE DIDN'T ELABORATE ON IT. ANYWAY WHEN WE LANDED, WE GOT OFF AND GOT OUR LUGGAGE. THAT'S WHEN WE HEARD THE NEWS THAT IT WAS DELTA FLIGHT 191 FROM FT. LAUDERDALE THAT HAD CRASHED. BUT IT WAS LIKE IT NEVER REGISTERED TO THEM THAT IT WAS OUR FLIGHT. IF THEY ACKNOWLEDGED ANY TYPE OF RELIEF OR THANKFULNESS THAT THEY WEREN'T ON THAT PLANE I NEVER SAW OR HEARD IT. IT WAS LIKE THEY JUST DIDN'T UN-DERSTAND. I CANT SAY THAT I WAS GRATEFUL EITHER AT THAT POINT BECAUSE I STILL GOT MY BUTT CHEWED OUT THE WHOLE WAY BACK HOME. I WAS AFRAID THAT MOM WAS GOING TO BE MAD AT ME BECAUSE WE HAD TO BUY

ANOTHER SET OF TICKETS FOR THE OTHER PLANE. I DON'T REMEMBER HOW MUCH THEY WERE, BUT I DO REMEMBER HER TELLING ME SHE COULDN'T WAIT TO TELL MOM. IT WAS A VERY LONG TRIP HOME.

WHEN WE GOT THERE, OF COURSE MOM WAS GLAD TO SEE ME AND AFTER SHE GAVE ME A BIG KISS AND A HUG I TOLD HER THAT MRS. B---WANTED TO SEE HER. MOM WENT OUTSIDE (Thinking Mrs. B----- would have a wonderful account of how they had missed death) BUT AS SOON AS SHE MET HER, MRS.B----- COMMENCED TO TELL HER WHAT A STUPID blank-blank-blank SHE HAD FOR

A DAUGHTER. IT WENT DOWN HILL FOR HER FROM THERE. "

Isn't that amazing! Do you know that this is exactly what the word of God says happens to people that are all about themselves and not about the love of God? Look at what the book of Romans has to say:

Because that, when they knew God, they glorified him not as God, neither were thankful; but became vain in their imaginations, and their foolish heart was darkened. Professing themselves to be wise, they became fools.
Rom 1:21-22

I bet that poor family is the kind of people that shake their fists at God and say, " I've never seen a miracle! God has never done anything for me!" and just like everyone else that says that, it's not because God has left them out, but because their foolish hearts are darkened.

I would say that they are a prime example of a truth that I often say....

Just because God does a miracle for you doesn't mean that you are smart enough to recognize it.

Let him that has an eye to see, see. And if not, then just go ahead and be mad.

Chapter
4

A New Eye to See

Speaking of having an eye to see, let me tell you about the most incredible healing miracle I have ever personally witnessed.

One of the greatest doors that God has opened up for us is, the ability to serve in the south Texas country known as "The Valley". It's as far south as you can go and still be in the United States.

There is not much that separates the U.S. from Mexico these days, just a filthy brown trickle that once roared all the way from Colorado and still is called the "Rio Grand". You stand at that muddy riverbed and what you see is the difference between a blessing and a curse. There is an invisible separation between hope and hopelessness that is much more than that tiny river. Much more than the few feet that separate the two, has been a spiritual hedge around a nation blessed by a merciful God. It's an amazing thing to stand and look at.

An Extreme Kind of Place

Brownsville, Texas is the last stop before crossing the border. Like most border towns, it's an extreme kind of place. Tens of thousands of teenagers and college kids flock there and to nearby South Padre Island for spring break every year. It's a good place to get into trouble. It's a good place to buy dope and pick up some women. It's the kind of place that can be extremely good for you or extremely bad for you, depending on where you are at and what you are there for. It's a great place for God to move.

I love places like that because God loves to do radical things in radical places. Extreme cultures tend to sift out the Christian pansies producing an extreme kind of church. I've seen it in New Orleans, we know it to be true in L.A. and the church in Brownsville is no exception; extreme. Extremely hungry for the presence of God. Extremely committed to reaching the lost. Excessive in praise and worship. Over the top in reaching out and making a difference. My kind of people. Some would say radical. I like the word radical, but I think Jesus would say zealous. (See 1 Cor 14:12, Titus 2:14 and Rev 3:19)

Now, the church that we are hooked up with down there is a little body called Mission Devina. The pastor there not only pioneered and maintains that work in Brownsville, but he also starts and supports many churches on the Mexican side as well. He does it because they are such awesome servants, and are so radical about finding the presence of God. Because they face such extreme hardship and circumstance, these churches are fertile ground for miracles. It is also the home of the greatest healing miracle I have ever seen to this day.

An Nervous Kind of Service

In the heat of summer, in the year 2000, Pastor Gene took our missions team across the border to minister at

a little church in Matamoras. After a brief intro-
duction, we began by leading in praise and worship.
By the end of the first song, I began to get a little
nervous. The congregation seemed to be more into
sizing us up than entering into the Spirit. I understand
how that works. There is no telling how many
American ministries have blown into town, pulled off-
the-wall stunts and promised everybody a Cadillac if
they would just have faith. I felt like there was
probably a good reason for their suspicion.

At the end of the first song, there was nothing but
polite applause. So I stopped what I was doing, turned
my total attention to the Lord and just acted like I was
at home crying out to God. Nobody but me and Jesus
in the house. We began to play "In Moments Like
These" and the presence of Holy Spirit came like an invisible AC unit that had just been cranked on. No
longer aware of the incredible heat in that tiny building,
I began to since a great move of God stirring the room.
As we continued to play the song, the room began to
get loud. People began to stand up and something
began to happen.

At first, just a person here and then another person
there, began to verbalize praise in Spanish. Then
another would begin to sob uncontrollably. Then
several people at one time, until finally the hundreds
that were crammed into this room began to shout at the
top of their lungs, arms lifted, eyes filled with tears and
God began to do His thing.

I had never been to this church before. I didn't know if
this was standard procedure or what. I couldn't understand what people were saying to the pastor as he

went from one person to another throughout the room.
All I knew was that the presence of God was so
tangible and so self-evident, all I could do was continue
to sing and play my guitar as this went on for more
than an hour. My sermon went out the window and it
was just a radical time of praise and brokenness before
the Lord.

An Extreme Kind of Miracle

After things began to die down, the pastor took the
podium as another pastor there began to explain to me
in broken English that many people had been phys-
ically healed of many different things that night. I said,
"That's great!" as I went to step out a side door to get
some fresh air. As I did, I bumped my head on the
concrete wall, not realizing that the door was only
about five and half feet tall. It was a homemade job
that might have been a hundred years old. All I could
do was hope that not many people saw it. Oh I hate it
when that happens! As I tended to the "goose egg" on
the top of my head, the pastor invited people to come
and give their testimonies. Within just a minute, there
were lots of people in line.

This one had been healed of a fever, that one had been
healed of a migraine. At this point I was praying for
some of that on me. Everyone was clapping and
cheering with excitement such that I can't really put into
print. This was the revival that they had been praying
for and I was blessed to be there the very first day.

I was talking to one of my missions team, when I
noticed the room got very quiet as an older lady elo-
quently and softly gave her testimony. Later it was
explained to me that this lady had been a member of

this church since she was a child. In her early teenage years she began loosing her eyesight as a result of undiagnosed diabetes. By the time she did get treatment, she had completely gone blind and had continued to serve the church the best she could in quiet holiness and faithful attendance. The church knew her well.

She said that during the 2nd song we had played, she felt the Holy Spirit come upon her in a very unusual way. A moment later, she said that she began to see a vision and that it was the first time in many years she had seen anything. But after a few minutes, she began to realize that maybe this was not a vision at all. She calmly spoke through the microphone as a brother translated for me saying, "Now you know me and you know that I am blind." As God as my witness, that woman pointed at a lady sitting on the front row and said, "If I am so blind, then how can I see you?". Then she pointed to another saying "and you.... and you and you". The church was blown away! Right there with my wife, Pastor Gene Izzaguire and other members of my team present, we saw a woman healed of blindness and no man can take credit for it! None of us even laid a hand on her. It was just a special miracle time of healing. The Lord blessed her, and all of us there, with a miracle healing of blindness.

Since then, there have been dark times in my walk when I have been tempted to doubt God's healing touch. Every time I do, I remember the night in Matamoras when a little lady got healed of her blindness and I was there to see it. If you are somebody that desperately needs a miracle, I want to tell you that Jesus is the real deal and He still is in the miracle working business.

The Message in the Miracle

Sometimes a special move of God is not taught, it's caught. You have to be led by the Spirit, to be at a certain place at a certain time, in order for a certain miracle to happen. You have to be on the scene when the move of God happens. I know a lot of times we Christians are M.I.A. or even A.W.O.L. when General Jesus shows up to knock out our enemies.

In Acts Chapter 2, we read that 120 had stuck out the whole 10 days in the upper room even though thousands had been commanded to be there. It was those 120 people that the Holy Spirit fell upon and changed their lives. I tend to think that a lot of people don't see the miracle they need because they are not there when the miracle shows up.

I wonder how many times the devil tried to stop that woman from going to church that night. I wonder how many bad things happened that day that tempted her to just stay home. I wonder if she was tempted to leave when she found out a "gringo" would be preaching that night and not her pastor. I have no doubt that this poor blind woman had many legitimate reasons to not be among the worshippers that night. Had she played any one of those cards, she would still be blind today.

When we go to church, we need to go prepared for the Lord to show up in a special way. Our hearts need to be ready for whatever God wants to do within us and to us. I might get healed. Fine. I might get convicted. Fine again. I might get encouraged or even enlightened with some new revelation. That's all the more fine, but whatever Jesus wants to do, I'll leave that up to Him. It is my job to show up and my job to be prepared.

Sometimes you have to have a right heart, and be at the right place, for the right miracle to happen. Consider this new twist when you read this very familiar passage of scripture.

"Then the kingdom of heaven shall be likened to ten virgins who took their lamps and went out to meet the bridegroom. Now five of them were wise, and five were foolish. Those who were foolish took their lamps ar.d took no oil with them, 4 but the wise took oil in their vessels with their lamps. But while the bridegroom was delayed, they all slumbered and slept. And at midnight a cry was heard: 'Behold, the bridegroom is coming; go out to meet him!' "Then all those virgins arose and trimmed their lamps. And the foolish said to the wise, 'Give us some of your oil, for our lamps are going out.' "But the wise answered, saying, 'No, lest there should not be enough for us and you; but go rather to those who sell, and buy for yourselves.' "And while they went to buy, the bridegroom came, and those who were ready went in with him to the wedding; and the door was shut. Afterward the other virgins came also, saying, 'Lord, Lord, open to us!' "But He answered and said, 'Assuredly, I say to you, I do not know you.' "Watch therefore, for you know neither the day nor the hour in which the Son of Man is coming."
Matt 25:1-13 NKJV

God's miracles always have to do with perfect timing. That brings me to my next miracle.

Chapter
5

Perfect Timing

I have had the incredible privilege of preaching in at least 50 different prisons in several different countries, but most of them right here in Texas. Texas has everything when it comes to prisons. We've got every extreme imaginable, from work restitution centers where guys get out on the weekends, to monster walled castles that make the Shawshank Redemption look like the Ritz Carlton.

With some of them, you have to remind yourself that you're in a prison, while others you have to remind yourself that you're going to get out in an hour or two. Some of them are really scary, all of them dangerous, but every one a place where miracles can happen. On a hot summer day in July of 1995, I saw God work a miracle that has to do with "perfect timing".

A Captive Audience

There are different gifts and anointings from God for different kinds of ministry.

For instance, there is a different kind of anointing on me when I preach behind a pulpit than when I preach on the street. It's the same way for doing outreaches and missions work. God shows up in different ways when you do different kinds of work in His service.

I love prison ministry because you can always count on a life-changing move of God when you preach the mercy of Jesus to men that have not had mercy on others. Prison ministry is about loving people that everybody hates and remembering people that everybody wants to forget. That's radical, that's Jesus, and it's fertile ground for miracles.

Now, I am no political liberal that doesn't understand the need for prisons. When you get there, hang out for a while and meet the inmates. You will leave there saying, "Thank God for prisons!" That's the truth, but the balance of a natural policy that says, "If you do the crime - you do the time", should be church policy that says, "If you do the crime you'll do the time ---- and I will show you Jesus." There is nothing like a "captive audience".

Jailhouse Religion

Most of the church fails to recognize the revival that has been going on behind the bars of this country. One of the greatest moves of God that has happened in the United States over the past twenty years has gone on, not within the four walls of the church, but behind the walls with barbed wire on top.

I have had a lot of people ask me about the sincerity of prisoners when they receive Jesus and become committed to the chapel services. They say, " Don't you think a lot of them are just playing games?" My response to that is, since I have been pastoring, I have never seen a service yet where somebody wasn't playing games. It doesn't keep me from preaching on Sundays, so why should it keep me from preaching in prisons?

The next way I would respond to that is by saying that the still, small voice that is described in 1 Kings 19:12 is not just a description of the way God speaks. Still and small would also be a description of the heart that hears the voice of God.

Prison is a place where you get still. Your life is put on hold. You starve to be busy doing anything. Prison is a place where you get small. No matter how tough you are, there are ten guys tougher than you every 50 feet. It is a place of disappointment, shame and heartache. Prison is the perfect environment for a move of God.

The reason why so many men and women get saved and turned onto Jesus in prison is because, for the first time they are still and small, and for the first time they recognize the voice of the Lord. For the first time they are humble and heart broken; a place where God can do great things!

A Man Against the Wall

Near the tiny town of Tennessee Colony, way back in the piney woods of East Texas, lies some of the states most notorious prisons. Many of them have reputations of being what inmates call "Gladiator Farms". Places where you learn to fight or die. Others, because of the work of selfless chaplains and ministers, have reputations of being a place you can really find the Lord.

The Michael Unit is a prison that I have heard all kinds of terrible things about. Not just from the inmates, but from the guards as well. I spoke to a young man at a unit in Abilene that had worked as a guard at the Michael Unit for 2 years. He spent a full half hour telling me one horror story after another. By anybody's standard it's a rough place, but I'll tell you that, in the mid nineties, there was a great move of God that happened there.

I was invited to preach there on a Friday. When I got to the tiny chapel within the prison, I was surprised to find it completely full with standing room only. There was music playing. People were worshiping the Lord and there was a general feeling of expectation, like God was going to do something big. All the pews were full. It looked like there was just enough room between two men standing against a wall by the stage, that I might be able to get out of the way until it was my turn to get up there. I nudged my big self in between these two guys as they politely tried to make room for me. I opened up my Bible and rested it on top of my guitar case that was standing upright in front of me. On that ratty, old guitar case was a big red bumper sticker that my wife had picked up for me in San Francisco. It said "ALCATRAZ: School of hard knocks"

Standing to my right and pressed up against me was a man that looked a lot older than he actually was. He had been singing like everybody else when I began to squeeze my way next to the wall. He worshiped the Lord, and as he did, big tears rolled down his face, past a very obvious scar on his cheek. The scar proved that he had done his share of fighting and the tears proved he had surrendered to Jesus.

After a moment of praise, the song was finished and the band got ready to change songs. The man to my right was holding a Bible and he changed hands with it, to shake mine. I couldn't help but notice the cover on that Bible. A lot of times, guys in prison will get to work leather and get really good at that kind of artwork. Big leather Bible covers with incredibly intricate designs are popular among the Christians in prisons. This cover was one of the best looking ones I had ever seen. "Did you make that?", I asked. "Yes", he said, happy that I noticed. "This Bible is really special to me and I wanted it to have a nice cover." "Really nice", I replied. "I'm gonna be here a long time", he went on to say, "and I wanted a good cover so's I don't wear my Bible out." Then he said it again, "I'm going to be here a long time."

Now I made it a rule to never ask an inmate what he is in there for and I wasn't about to break that rule then. Instead of asking him why he was going to be in prison for a long time, I decided to ask him why that Bible was so special to him. He began to tell me that Bible was a gift from his brother, a brother that he had not seen in a long time.

The Roots of a Lifetime Sentence

For the next ten minutes I became oblivious to the service in the chapel because all my attention went into what this man was telling me. The Holy Spirit really touched my heart as the young man casually and honestly poured his out.

He said that he had been a curse to his family all of his life. He explained that he was raised in a good home, with good parents, and several brothers and sisters. No matter what they had tried to do for him though, he still ended up in trouble. Trouble at school, trouble at home, trouble on the streets; and he said he enjoyed every minute of it. He told me that there was no end to the terrible things he had put his family through. He had stolen from all of them. He had threatened every one of them.

He began to get arrested for little things at first and then bigger things later on. The year he should have graduated high school, he did something terrible that would land him in prison for the rest of his life. He said that the day he got sentenced, he threatened the judge's life and as he got escorted out of the courtroom he could see his family, brothers and sisters weeping and huddled all together.

He told me that everyone had visited him and at first those visitations were very frequent. An older brother would see him at least once a month and every time he came, he would try to talk to him about Jesus. My friend with the Bible cover didn't want to hear anything about Jesus in those days.

Several years went by, and matters got worse, when a fight he got into landed him in the hospital and his combatant into the morgue. Even though it was found to be self-defense by the inquiry, the friends of the person he killed vowed revenge. Because of that he was moved from one prison to another, before winding up in the Michael Unit. Even though these prisons were hundreds of miles apart, his brother continued his monthly visit and continued to share Jesus.

Ten years past by and he was now meaner than ever. He no longer looked forward to his brother's visits, but he ridiculed him and hated his Christian agenda. He told me the last time he saw his brother, he threatened his life saying that if he tried to talk to him about Jesus again, he would rip his tongue from out of his head! With that he spit in his brother's face and told him to leave and to take his Jesus with him.

He said he really thought his brother would show up the next month but he didn't, in fact, that had happened three years ago and he hadn't seen him since.

I pointed to his Bible and made reference to the chapel we were standing in. "So what changed? When did you get saved?"

His family had finally given up on him. There were several years where there was no contact at all. He understood how all that went and figured he had it coming. That last Christmas he had gotten a package in the mail and when he opened it, he found a large print, New King James Bible, with the words of Jesus imprinted in red. Inside the cover he found the simple inscription,

'Read the red letters'.

As he walked back to his cell trying to make what the inscription was all about, another inmate attacked him. The fight lasted for little more than a minute before the guards were there. Lucky for him, because this guy was trying to kill him. A fight in prison will land you in administrative segregation and the only thing he had

to do while he was isolated from all the other prisoners
was to read that book; particularly the red letters.

He had been saved, set free and a big part of the church
in that prison for more than 8 months now. God had
done something that only God could do. He gave him
a right mind and a new heart. He really was a new
man. The change was miraculous.

The problem he had now was that he was afraid to tell
his family. His was afraid that after all the terrible
games he had played with his brother, they might
suspect that this was just another one of his tricks. He
wanted his brother to really know that his life had been
changed and that he really was a new creature in
Christ, but how could he prove that in prison?

As he asked me this question, the Chaplin began to introduce me and it was time for me to preach. With
only a moment left, I prayed a simple prayer with him
that the Lord would do a miracle and show his brother
that he really was saved in a powerful way.
We hugged, I preached and I've never seen him since.

Peanuts, Hotdogs and a Miracle

The next day, some 250 miles west of Tennessee
Colony, I found myself at a long awaited baseball game
at the ballpark in Arlington. A scalper in the parking
lot sold me and my friend, two el-primo seats right
behind 3rd plate.

Now, being a fat man, when I sat in the chair, a lot of
me spilled over onto the two people next to me. My
good friend Maurice didn't mind and as God would

have it, the guy on my other side was a skinny man, who had lots of room. We politely said "hi" and then we put our attention to the ballgame.

In the sixth inning, Benji Gil hit a ball so hard, it fouled out in the 3rd deck behind us. At the sound of the crack of the bat I shouted "Praise God!", convinced it would go out of the park. I was yelling before I knew it was going to go foul. When I squeezed myself back into the chair, the stranger next to me said, "So you're a Christian?"

That began a polite conversation about the two of us being saved and both of us being lay ministers. I told him that besides being the youth pastor at the church I was with, I did a lot of prison ministry. I remember him turning to his wife and saying, "Hey honey, this guy preaches in prisons."

After a moment, he leaned over so that he didn't have to speak so loud saying, "I don't usually tell people this, but I have a brother in prison."

"Oh really", I asked, "what prison is he in?"

"The Michael Unit" he replied.

"That's Funny, I was just at the Michael Unit last night."

He leaned the other way and said, "Hey Honey, this guy was preaching at the Michael Unit just last night."

"There were a lot of guys in the church service", I offered, " maybe I saw him."

"No you wouldn't see him in any church service," he said with a sad look, " The last time I tried to pray with him he spit in my face & threatened to pull my tongue out!"

A Homerun for Jesus

That's when it hit me that something else was going on besides the ballgame. In the midst of tens of thousands of people, I began to wake up to the fact that a serious move of God was happening. A sat there silently, with my jaw dropped, as this stranger began to tell the same exact story I had heard the night before. He told me that he had been faithful for more than ten years to visit his curse of a brother. He talked about the pain and the regret he felt for giving up on his little brother. He knew that God could do a miracle and save him, but after so many years of him playing games, he just didn't know how. He said that he had decided to get on with his life, and then he confessed that he was sorry he didn't do anything after that.

"But you did do something." I said as the Holy Ghost began to move on both of us, "You sent him a Bible at Christmas and more than that, he read it, got saved and has been a big part of the church for more than 8 months!"

"What!", this man exclaimed in disbelief.

"Listen, last night I heard the same exact story from your brother, who happened to stand by me before I preached and we prayed that God would do a miracle and prove to you that he really was saved. The next day, in a different part of the state, I bump into you, not knowing who you are, when I could have sat by any of these other tens of thousands of people. This is a miracle! What are the odds that you and I would happen to meet at this time and at this place? Does your brother have a scar on his left cheek?"

"Yes" he said with tears.

"Is he this tall and ugly as a goat?"

"That would be him." He said shaking his head.

"Well big brother, the Lord has honored your prayers and your ministry to your brother in prison. I believe the Lord has sent us here together as an answer to your brother's prayer that you would know it." By now his wife, who had been setting there with her hand over her mouth, had both of her hands on her husband's shoulder. "My God," she said with tears, "It really is a miracle!"

"My brother is saved?" he asked, wanting to confirm what he was hearing. "How did that happen?

In the midst of ten thousands of people and a nationally televised ballgame I confirmed what an incredible thing had, and even was then, taking place. I smiled as big as I could and told him,

"He read the red letters!"

The Message in the Miracle

God is a God of perfect timing. One of the great things about being led by the Spirit of the Lord is that He causes you to be at the right place, at the right time, for the right miracle to happen. I heard the great speaker and pastor T.D. Jakes say at one of his Manpower Conventions, that some of the life changes that the Lord has for us can't be taught, they have to be caught. I know that's a fact. In other words, you have to be at the right place to get your life changed. I have heard Mike Murdock say that being obedient to the Spirit of God lands us at the right place and at the right time. I know it's the truth as I pointed out in the previous chapter.

The pool of Bethesda, the 120 in the upper room and the parable of the 5 wise virgins are just three biblical examples of this principle. (John 5:4, Acts 2:1, Matthew 25:10)

You could have heard Noah's teaching on the flood for a hundred and twenty years, but unless you were standing in the ark the day the door closed, you would have missed the miracle of being saved. You just had to be there.

For those who are willing to walk with God and be led by His Spirit, He makes sure that we are there when we need to be there. Right now might be a good time to pray and ask the Lord to lead you. Ask God to set you up for a blessing and have you at the right place and at the right time. Your miracle will be waiting when you get there!

"The steps of a good man are ordered by the LORD:
and he delighteth in his way. Though he fall,
he shall not be utterly cast down:

for the LORD upholdeth him with His hand.
Psalms 37:23 KJV

You can hear this testimony from a live service in Matamoras, Mexico by simply going to the Open Door webpage and clicking on the image of me. It's marked, "Hear a special message from pastor Troy". It's just a few minutes before it gets into the live recording and all you have to do is point and click. No need to download anything.

www.opendoorministries.org

There is one other thing I think about when I remember this incredible miracle. I wonder if maybe the scalper I met in the parking lot might have been an angel? It might be a while before I know.

Chapter
6

Another Miracle at Entebbe Airport

I'm not scared of a whole lot of things. Not that I'm not scared of anything, because I get freaked out like anybody. Let's see, I'm scared of heights, really loud noises, women with guns, you know, things that are logical. But, the thought of being somewhere with no access to food has tended to terrify me in years past. This is what I thought we were facing on our first missions trip to Uganda, East Africa.

I had no idea that the people were going to be so wonderful, or that that the food would be so available and delicious. I really didn't know anything about Uganda, except that I had never seen a fat man from there and that made me think I had better go prepared.

Now, my mother had dreamed her entire life of going to Africa. When my wife and I had a door open for us to go, we invited mom along for the ride. She was the perfect person to take with me, because I figured between Leanna and mom there was no way I could go hungry.

Mom and I prepared for our two weeks in Uganda by bringing two suitcases loaded with food. I'm talking about several pounds of Beef Jerky & at least a dozen of those really neat tuna fish kits that come with crackers. We had four or five bags of potato chips, a few loaves of bread and lots of cans of SPAM. More than looking like missionaries, we took on the persona of traveling salesmen for the Hormel meat company. If it was meat in a can, we had it in our suitcases. The way I saw it was, if we were going to suffer for Jesus, it was not going to be for lack of food.

Raid on Entebbe

Entebbe Airport is an amazing place if you're any kind of a history buff, particularly if you're a lover of Israel. In 1976, Entebbe's airport was the site of a raid by Israeli commandos called "Operation Thunderball". They freed 103 Israeli hostages from a plane hijacked by Palestinian terrorists that night & it was nothing short of a military miracle. Against all odds they landed 4 planes, killed the terrorists, rescued the hostages and escaped to Kenya nearly unscathed. From the airport tower a terrorist's bullet hit the back of a brave soldier named Yoni Netanyahu. He was the one military casualty that night. He died on the tarmac. Yoni was the older brother of a young man named Benjamin Netanyahu, who later became Prime Minister of Israel. For more information concerning this event I suggest you go to the official Israeli defense forces website and read up on what happened. You can find it at this web address:

www.idf.il/english/history/entebbe1.stm

So when I stepped or I should say staggered off of our triple seven that day, I was thinking of Yoni and the cannibalistic dictator Idi Amin and Operation Thunderball. We were exhausted from a ten and a half hour flight to London from DFW, a sixteen-hour layover in England and another ten-hour flight from London to Kampala, Uganda. As tired as we were, we were also thrilled to be in Africa and excited to be at the airport of Israel's famous miracle.

Smugglers' Blues

Because we were at the back of the plane, we were the last ones in line to go through customs. We saw very quickly that things were done differently here than at the customs in DFW, Texas. No surprise there. It was not a matter of "**if**" your luggage gets looked at, it was a matter of "**how it gets searched**". What you are supposed to do is, put your luggage on one of the many available tables, open it up and wait for a soldier to go through them. In this same room are sharp dressed Ugandan soldiers, most of them female, positioned everywhere with automatic machine guns. If you get a nice soldier, he or she will not show the room your fancy underwear. If you get somebody that's in a bad mood, you can expect to repack everything that has not been confiscated. It's just part of the African experience.

Now, while we are waiting our turn to be pillaged, I couldn't help but notice the interesting signs posted everywhere. Interesting because every sentence was in multiple languages, because Uganda is divided with scores of tribes and dialects even today. Everything posted reminded me of the beginning of a Gideon Bible. I am sure that the combination of jet lag and general stupidity is what kept all of us from reading the signs in English, but it didn't occur to me until just before my turn in line, what the signs actually said. I mean, why look at the English words when there are so many other cool languages to look at? When my blood shot eyes finally did read the English words, it was like a hammer on my head, which awakened me from my casual coma. To my horror, it dawned on me what this sign was saying in so many different languages:

"IT IS A CRIME TO SMUGGLE ANY KIND OF MEAT INTO UGANDA PUNISHABLE BY IMPRISONMENT".

"Excuse me?" I thought. Can this be right? We didn't just have meat. We had two entire suitcases of contraband SPAM. My eyes darted around the room and I saw how they tolerated things that were not allowed into the country. They didn't. My immediate thought was that I did not plan on our ministry to Uganda to be a prison ministry. Especially since my wife and my mom were with me.

Leanna looked at me and could tell something was wrong. So did a female soldier standing a few feet away from me. I didn't know it, but I was attracting the attention of a woman with a gun who was trained to seek out people that are unusually nervous.

I whispered to mom and pointed at the sign. Her blood left her face and at that point she began to speak in tongues. This was a good time to "who-ka-ma-sie" and "shun-die". I had visions of running back out to the plane yelling, "Run, Leanna, run!" There was nothing I could do.

"Hello, sir", said a deep voice behind me. I turned to stand toe-to-toe with the lady that had been watching me. "Is there a problem?", she asked.

A Woman With a Gun

I wanted to say lots of things, all at the same time. I wanted to explain that we had never been to Uganda before and that we didn't realize until now that it was illegal to bring food into the country. I wanted to tell her that somehow all of the missionaries we had talked to before this day had failed to warn us that we might have this kind of problem. I wanted to add also that it really wasn't their faults either because they probably didn't bring half of a convenience store with them. I wanted to answer her question in a way that was right and didn't alarm her. As tension built up within me, I got ready to speak. But again to my horror, instead of saying anything intelligent, I blurted out the first thing that came to mind.

"Hi'dy", was all I could manage. As soon as I said it, I just stood there and smiled, adding to my stupidity. Johnson County, Texas had taken me over. It was a pitiful moment.

"Hi'dy?", she asked a bit taken back. Then in a heavy African tone she asked, "What is Hi'dy?"

I said, "You know; how ya doing, good to see ya; it's short for howdy."

"From where is your dialect?", she demanded.

Thinking of the suitcase of food, I thought she asked, "What is your diet?", and started to ramble on how that I would eat just about anything.

She interrupted me and said, "No, I mean where are you from?"

"Oh, I'm sorry", I said laughing a little. "I'm from Texas and "hi'dy" is a common greeting there."

All of a sudden she lit up like a Christmas tree. Her entire countenance changed from serious to surprised and happy. "You are from Texas?", she asked through a perfectly white smile. "Where the Cowboys live?"

I answered her question in a round about way and she began to tell me that she and her friend were going to college in Kampala and that they were having to write a paper on Texas.

She said, " I love your manner of speech, please say something else." Now remember she's the one with the gun, so I mustered up the hick'est accent I could manage and started saying things like, "Somebody poisoned my waterin' hole!"

"Yes, Yes! That is Texas!", she shouted. "You must meet my friend. She will be so happy to greet you."

And with that, she began to lead us through customs. I motioned at mom to follow. Leanna and I picked up our suitcases, and out of customs the three of us went. She marched us right out without looking through a solitary bag!

On the other side of the airport, she introduced me to her friend and we politely talked about the great state of Texas. She was blown away.

"I have always wanted to go there", she said " We study you in school."

With that, we walked out of the airport to meet the people that were waiting on us, suitcases in tow behind us. When we told them what had happened, they marveled, saying that absolutely nobody gets through Entebbe Airport without customs going through your bags. Nobody! Much less three people getting through with "illegal" contraband. Spam or not, it was still illegal and the Lord had done an incredible miracle for the three of us.

From Entebbe we had a long 5-hour drive through the jungle to the city of Fort Portal, on the border of Congo. We had a long time to think about what God had done for us that day. One of the funny things that had struck me was that, in Texas, the school kids of Johnson County study about the pigmies of Uganda. At the same exact time, the pigmies in Uganda are studying about the people of Johnson County! The world is a strange place.

The Message in the Miracle

"For in the day of trouble
he will keep me safe in his dwelling;
he will hide me in the shelter of his tabernacle
and set me high upon a rock."
Psalms 27:5

That's what happened that day. He hid us in the safety
of His presence. As I have already told you, I have
seen the Lord do a miracle and make blind eyes see.
Here is a miracle where the Lord made seeing eyes
blind! He can do the same for you. I believe that God
is hiding you right now from untold troubles and
horrors. When the child molester comes to your neigh-
borhood, let him not be able to see your children.
When the terrible virus comes to your place of work,
let it not be able to find your lungs! Right now would
be a good time to openly thank the Lord that He hides
you from your enemies.

Praise God!

Chapter
7

Miracles and the Wedgwood Shooting

Sept 15, 1999 was a Wednesday night and our little church was getting ready for our midweek service. I had just plugged my guitar in and was about to or "fix'n to" as we say, fire things up, when someone told me for the first time, that there had been a shooting at Wedgwood Baptist Church in south Fort Worth.

I immediately knew what church it was. I had seen it many times. It was less than ten miles away from us and just a stone's throw from our drummer's house. The reports at first were foggy, as they always are. At that point all we knew was that a gunman walked into the church and shot up the place. It was feared some were dead.

We started our service with prayer for the Wedgwood Baptist Church, as did other churches all over the country that night. As soon as the service was over, we all ran to our televisions to find out what we could. The local news was on literally all night long as new reports came in. There were people dead, most of them kids. There were others fighting for their lives and others that might not ever walk again. It was a terrible time for so many wonderful people.

Maybe you have heard about the famous shootings at
Wedgwood Baptist Church and the awful events that
took place there as they were reported literally around
the world. Maybe you were amazed at the ability of
their Pastor, Al Meridith, as he spoke the power of God
into every microphone that was put into his face.
Maybe you have heard of the tragedy, but have not
heard of the miracles that took place as those gunshots
rang out.

When you look at the events of that terrible night you
can see more than the work of a demon possessed killer
bent on killing as many Christians as he could bag. A
closer look will show the signature of somebody else
that was there that night, somebody that was doing
miracles.

The Persecuted Church

Persecution is a big part of the church today. According to
Voice of the Martyrs (*www.persecution.com*), more
Christians were killed in the twentieth century for their
faith in Jesus than in all 19 centuries before now,
combined. I am familiar with some of the hell that the
body of Christ is being put through today. It is es-
timated that at least 45 million Christians were put to
death during the twentieth century alone, and that
somewhere around seventy million Christians have
been martyred since a deacon named Stephen was
stoned to death in Jerusalem, as recorded in the biblical
book of Acts.

The Lord has allowed me to be friends with pastors all
over the world. Many of them are persecuted in
terrible ways. My good friend Suddeer Muhanty, and

his wonderful congregation in India, have suffered through bombs going off in their services planted by Muslims and Hindus. My precious brother, K.L Dickson in Uganda East Africa has narrowly escaped with his life on several occasions as Muslims have come into his services with machine guns, and if it had not been for a miracle move of God, he would not have lived to tell about it. My good friend Gene Izzaguira in Brownsville, Texas has had the Mexican Mafia after him for years. One time in deep Mexico, some radical Catholics hung him and his friend from a tree, telling him that they would kill him unless he swore his God was the Virgin of the Guadalupe. He wouldn't do it and before they were going to put him to death, he told the chief of the Indians that were hanging them there, that God would hold him responsible for their death. After some time of argument, the chief commanded the priest to let Pastor Gene go, which they did; but not before they beat him with the blunt end of machetes.

This kind of stuff goes on every single day all over the world. Why should we Americans think that we will never suffer persecution? If you've got Jesus, that makes you a target by an increasingly large number of people all over the world. You better batten down the hatches and understand that this is part of it, because persecution will increase in the years to come.

While the persecution we face as Americans is not near as often as in other countries, it's just as real. A more subtle form that we face is in our own news services, and it was very evident during the reporting of this terrible event.

I was amazed at the liberal media as they fumbled
around in stupidity after the Wedgwood shootings.
They would look into the camera and say things like,
"After all the investigations, there still seems to be no
motive for this tragedy." I bet I heard the term "no
motive" a hundred times in the weeks following
September 15th.

A guy walks into a youth service yelling, "Christianity
is B.S.!" and shoots a ton of people that are wor-
shipping Jesus and remarkably the media can't find a
motive. Can you imagine the same thing happening
not in a Baptist church, but a gay bar, and the media
declaring that they were puzzled to find a motive?
Think about it. If somebody walked into a gay bar,
yelled various remarks about homosexuals and shot
people at point blank range, can you imagine the media
being puzzled for a motive? No! There would be
nothing but a parade of experts and special reports on
the persecution of homosexuals. The motive would be
understood and clearly defined as mindless persecution
and declared to be a hate crime. Protests would be
staged, laws would be passed, and outrage would be
thrown onto every American for anything perceived as
lack of tolerance for homosexuality.

While the TV and newspapers were saturated with information about the shootings, those things never
happened for the Christians that were murdered at
Wedgwood because the media couldn't find a motive.
Now when they say they couldn't find a motive, I
believe what they meant to say was that they couldn't
find where the people of Wedgwood had provoked the
attack. After all, from the medias' point-of-view, these
people were Baptists, and we all know that it is at least

possible that these killings were provoked somehow. You draw your own conclusions about the liberal beast of our media today, but anybody with more than a few brain cells left can see what the motive was.

He was there to kill some Christians. Any Christian. It didn't matter what age or what gender. He was there to kill as many people that loved Jesus as he possibly could, but the Lord would have something to say about that.

Trial and Testing

"See-you-at-the-pole" is a worldwide event that was started just a few miles from where all of this happened. It's a student led prayer that happens around the flagpole at high schools all over the world. A day for the Christian kids to show their solidarity for each other and their witness to the rest of the school. It's a neat deal.

A lot of churches have special youth rallies the night of "see-you-at-the-pole" to celebrate Jesus and reach out to other kids. That is what was going on the night of September 15th. It wasn't just a regular church service, it was a room full of teenagers gathered together that night, with hundreds showing up.

On the stage a band called "Forty Days" was playing. I believe prophetically that spiritually spoke of the time of trial and testing these powerful Christians were about to go through. The music was loud, the room was excited, and the kids were having a good time, when suddenly the world became a very different place for everyone present.

Larry Gene Ashbrook, a forty-seven year old jobless man known for violent rages and conspiracy writings, busted into that service yelling and cursing anything to do with Jesus. At the same time, he was pointing his pistol at bewildered teenagers everywhere and pulling the trigger. A ten-minute rampage followed that would leave seven dead and seven more shot before he sent a bullet through his own brain.

Pandemonium followed as frantic parents began to show up alongside ambulances and cameramen. Police and emergency medical personnel ran back and forth as victims were treated and the area secured. Phone lines became jammed as friends and family first became aware of the horrifying news.

Getting the World's Attention

The unthinkable had happened. For those of us in North Texas, it had happened at home. For the next several weeks, this single event would dominate anything that had to do with the media, particularly local media.

House Majority Leader Dick Armey issued a statement saying he "reacted with shock and horror". Calling it a tragic event in a "house of hope and love", Gov. George W. Bush, along with other officials, expressed shock and dismay. President Clinton called Pastor Al Meredith and spoke to him personally, while Vice-President Gore spoke to him on "Larry King Live". CNN would broadcast the memorial service live, along with other TV and Radio stations. Literally billions of people worldwide would see or hear something that had to do with Wedgwood Baptist Church.

But there is more. There was a lot that was not reported by the majority of talking heads. A lot of things happened in the midst of those shootings that were not tragic at all, but in fact, miraculous.

Someone Else Besides the Shooter Was Making Things Happen on That Evening.

Just before Larry Ashbrook walked into the room, he shot out some windows from outside. The place where he shot those windows out was right beside the children's playground. A playground that should have been filled with kids, but by the hand of God, was completely empty. Every single children's and preschool's class was running late that night and nobody had made it to the playground yet!

Teenagers didn't leave when the shooting first started because they thought that it might be part of a staged skit somehow. Lots of people reported thinking that the gun was firing blanks mostly because it just didn't seem real that people were being murdered in church. Drue Phillips, the nineteen year old bass player for the band Forty Days said, "We thought it was a joke, we knew a skit was going on later." But Drue and the rest of the band watched in horror as the gun was pointing at them and bullets began to fly onto the stage where they were standing. Though he fired repeatedly at them hitting all kinds of equipment and into the walls behind them, miraculously no band member was hit.

In the midst of the shooting, Ashbrook lit a homemade pipe bomb and threw it into the crowd of kids. They were starting to understand this was no joke.

Miraculously the bottom of the bomb fell off and it didn't blow up the way it was supposed to, sparing the lives of scores of kids.

As the killer walked back and forth through the room shouting obscenities and shooting at kids, a mother was desperately trying to force her mentally disabled 18-year-old daughter out of the pew and onto the floor. There was no way to calm her down and she made an easy target for the coward with the gun. Mary Beth Talley, a 17 year old who had ran into the room to warn everyone of the shooter, saw the struggle and lay on top of the handicapped girl as Ashbrook went to kill her. Mary Beth heard the shot and then she felt a sharp sting as a bullet entered into her back. Even after being shot, she held tight to the hand of the disabled girl and kept her calm while Ashbrook continued to look for vulnerable targets.

Unlike other kids in the room, Mary Beth had scoliosis. This condition that is a curse to so many, was in fact a blessing to this brave young lady. The curve in her spine directed the bullet away from her major organs and thus saved her life. She would recover and live to tell her testimony!

Kids bolted out when they could, others scrambled from pew to pew, most lay still trying not to draw attention, as Ashbrook killed seven people and wounded seven others. While most were wisely trying to protect themselves anyway they could, a young man with a troubled past and a biblical name sat up straight with his head bowed in prayer. "Lord,

Please let this end!" he prayed with his face in hands. His youth pastor and several others, all of them covered with blood, were pulling at his pant legs trying to get him to get under the pew. He sat still in prayer. As the Spirit of the Lord moved on this young man, the Lord would answer his prayer and end the bloodshed through none other than him. Jeremiah Neitz heard the shots, saw the slaughter, prayed the prayer, and then for

some inexplicable reason, jumped to his feet and confronted Ashbrook, not with his strong and muscular build, but with the love of God.

"Sir, what you need is Jesus Christ!", Jeremiah shouted as the gun was pointed at him. The demon inside of Ashbrook was outraged at this kind of a show and he began to yell and curse all the more.

"You can shoot me if you want", Jeremiah said with his arms to his sides, "but I know where I am going. I am going to heaven. How about you, sir?"

As mad as it made him, the love of God in Jeremiah's voice shut the gunman down. He answered his question by sitting down in a pew, putting the pistol to his head and sending himself to hell.

Nearby, Mary Beth who was still on top of her handicapped friend, Heather, heard Jeremiah's invitation and then heard the last shot ring out. Jeremiah would later say in a newspaper quote, "It had nothing to do with me, it was all God."

The Last Word

A lot of people think a lot of different things when they look back at what happened and what could have happened that Wednesday evening. The world is a lesser place because of the loss of the Christians that were murdered back then. People still suffer from the hurt that was inflicted on them for nothing more than gathering together in the name of Jesus. But for all the hurt and the loss, the story of Wedgwood is not just a story of tragedy, it is also a story of incredible triumph and proof that the Lord does not abandon His own.

The people of that powerful church will tell you, "Yes, some of us have died because of our faith in Jesus." But they will also tell you that they see the hand of God in the midst of the attack that came against them. Besides the things I have already stated, they will say things like this:

Though he fired 100 bullets into a crowd of over 400, only 14 were hit

An off-duty paramedic happened to be in the room and stabilized victims

None of the adults that died had any children

All seven victims were passionate and bold Christians

Through this, Pastor Al was able to personally pray with many world leaders, including President Clinton and then Governor Bush. Pastor Al would continue to have godly influence with George W. Bush when he became President of the United States.

The memorial service was aired live all over the world on CNN, including countries like Saudi Arabia, that do not allow the preaching of the Gospel within its borders. Because of the powerful word of God given in that service, people heard the Gospel and received Jesus that would have never otherwise had Jesus presented to them. Wedgwood has heard from people all over the world that were saved through that broadcast.

For every bullet fired against Christianity, millions of steps have been taken that move the cause of Christ forward. For every life lost through the shootings, thousands have been saved through the courage and testimony shown from the lives of those shot at. A lot more could be said and written about what God has done here, but I'll finish up by quoting Paul as recorded in Romans 1:8.

"I thank my God through Jesus Christ for all of you,
because your faith is being reported
all over the world."

The Message in the Miracle

There are so many messages that can be taught through these miracles, but I will focus on the miracle of young Jeremiah Neitz. Jeremiah would say in other interviews that he had come from a troubled past. His walk with the Lord was a brand new walk and he was still struggling with a lot of things. He was not a "churchy" kind of kid by anybody's standard, but when it came time for him to look down the barrel of a smoking gun, he stood side-by-side with Jesus Christ. Not knowing what he would say or how he would say it, he opened up his mouth and God took over.

I personally think a lot more than we will ever know was riding on Jeremiah's decision to be used of God in that chaotic moment. Jeremiah, no doubt, had done his share of fighting and he could have handled this very differently. Larry Gene Ashbrook was a sickly and weak looking little man, and there had to be some temptation to handle this the way Jeremiah would have handled this before he met Jesus.

By the power of the Holy Spirit, he answered Ashbrook's bullets, not with his muscles, but with the Jesus he had recently met. His muscles might have failed, but Jesus never fails. The word he spoke was powerful enough to stop the bullets and shut a mad man down. It was the perfect thing to say in that desperate moment and the only thing that could have been done to keep many, many others from being killed. With hundreds of kids crouching everywhere, Ashbrook still had 60 bullets left!

When it comes to persecution, the Bible gives us a special promise that was proven once again through the life of Jeremiah Neitz.

....do not be anxious beforehand about what you are to say, but say whatever is given to you in that hour; for it is not you who speaks, but it is the Holy Spirit. Mark 13:11-12 NAS

Or as Jeremiah would put it when he was asked about the word he spoke in that defining moment. "It was all God", he said.

Indeed it was, little brother. Indeed it was.

Chapter
8

An Off-the-Wall Miracle

The term "prophetic ministry" means different things to different people. I am not talking about an expert on the book of Revelation. I am talking about the ministry of being able to speak a prophetic word into somebody's life.

A pastor in Dallas has the greatest gift in prophetic anointing that I have ever seen. I have observed his ministry since 1986 and he consistently speaks prophetic words that come to pass. His name is Howard Richardson. He pastors a church called "Gates of Glory". I will talk more about this a little later.

Famous in Hell

Now, I have had lots of prophetic things spoken to me through the years. Some by people of God and some by the devil from hell. In a prison near Huntsville, Texas, I was invited to minister one-on-one to several inmates in solitary confinement. When I went to introduce myself to one individual, he interrupted me and said, "I know who you are, Troy Brewer! You're going to die a horrible death and blah blah blah..." He proceeded to pronounce curse after curse upon me and my family and spit right into the glass where my face was!

Mind you, I had never seen this man before in my life, but here he was calling me by name and pronouncing things that privately I was afraid of. To say I was startled is an understatement! He didn't know me, but the devil within him did.

I started yelling back at him, " You are not the author and the finisher of my faith!" I started quoting every "no fear" scripture I could think of, while he began to bang his head against the wall and say my name over and over again.

"A thousand shall fall at my left and ten thousand at my right hand, but it shall not come nigh me! No weapon formed against me shall prosper!", I yelled back at him.

I tuned him out and started rattling off the Word as fast as I could spit it out. We both made so much racket, a female guard ushered me out and back to the chaplain's office. I told them what had happened and they really didn't know what to think about it.

Some prison chaplains are more secular than Christian. Instead of being ministers, they run different helps programs. They invite ministers to come in. Some chaplains are not even Christian at all. I have seen Muslim chaplains and secular psychologist chaplains. This was a guy that didn't minister, but invited others to come in to minister for him. Now he was having a hard time believing me. They had trouble with that inmate all the time, but they had never seen him act like that before.

"Are you sure you have no contact with this man?" he asked with his eyebrow raised a little.

"I've never seen him before in my life", I said.

He asked, "Did you write anyone here and inform them you were coming?"

I replied, "I don't know any one here and my invitation was just from four days ago."

They scratched their head and said that they would call me. I never waited on the call. It's a good thing.

While his slanderous outburst caught me off guard and gave me the "heebee jeebees", I had a lot of time to think about what happened in that prison cell. It occurred to me on the three-hour drive home that night, that it's a good thing to be famous in hell.

The biblical seven sons of Sceva went to tackle a demon-possessed man, but they bit off more than they could chew. Having no relationship with Jesus, but trying to capitalize on the notoriety that Paul had as a preacher who rebuked the devil, these fools went toe-to-toe with a demon and without the power of Christ. They said "We command you in the name of Jesus that Paul preaches!"

Acts 19:15-17 records what happened next: *But the evil spirit answered them, "Jesus I know, and Paul I know; but who are you?" And the man in whom the evil spirit was leaped on them, mastered all of them, and overpowered them, so that they fled out of that house naked and wounded.* RSV

The devil's answer was that he had never heard of them. Not only did he beat the fire out of those poor guys, but he had his way to boot! The Bible says they left the house naked. Yikes! I've determined from this scripture it's good to be famous in hell.

I hope the devil wakes up every morning cussing me and goes to bed cussing me. I hope that your name is number two just under mine on the devil's top ten hit list! I hope that the very mention of your name brings to mind terrible disappointment and thoughts of opportunity lost to that cosmic punk. You bet I want to be famous in hell. To hell with the devil. May we be the itch he could never get scratched!

A Word From the Lord

Gates of Glory is not your normal church. They meet at different hotel ballrooms across the city of Dallas. You have to call their number to find out where the Sunday meeting is. For years it's been the same, (972-988-8708). During the week, brother Howard Richardson ministers throughout the country and even abroad, but he nearly always makes it back for a Sunday service in Dallas. He airs a weekly television show on the Daystar network.

Of course brother Howard is no normal pastor either. He preachers a very deep and in-your-face kind of word that doesn't do much for the feel good seekers that have invaded our churches. A lady plays the keyboards the whole time he preaches and when he gets done, he tends to read people's mail. He calls people out of the audience and gives them very specific and personal words from the Lord that correct and edify people's socks off. It's an incredible ministry that has touched tens of thousands.

He has spoken a lot of words into my life over the years. I heard a very wise man once say that the ministry you respect is the ministry that changes your life. I see brother Howard as kind of a spiritual father to me, because it was him that first declared I would preach the Gospel all over the world. When he said it, I was just a mixed up 19-year-old kid, at a tent meeting in Grand Prairie, Texas. So I do respect his ministry a lot. It has changed my life.

Remember, the ministry you respect is the ministry that changes your life. I have seen people in my own ministry hang around others that spoke bad about Leanna and I. As soon as they lost respect for us, our ministry had no more impact on their lives. That's the way the devil will use a goat in any church, anywhere. Make sure that you are not a goat. If you've got something bad to say about your pastor, tell it to him or tell it to the Lord, otherwise keep your mouth shut. What you see as blowing off steam can be a powerful tool in the hand of the enemy. I have known a lot of people that I wish had understood that principle. Paling-up with friends in the church and talking bad about a minister that has some form of spiritual authority over them or ministry into their life, is a great way to sever the power of God going into that life.

A Big Fish

It was a Sunday night and pastor Howard had just finished preaching.

"Lift those hands to the Lord and help me praise Him", He said.

After several minutes of seeking the Lord, he called me by name and prophesied the strangest thing.

He said, "Troy, when I see you, the Lord shows me something really off-the-wall. I see you catching a great big fish somewhere and when you catch it, the Lord is saying that this is a sign unto you that your ministry is not going to be a little bitty ministry, but a great big ministry."

What the heck is that all about, I thought! I am an off-the-wall kind of guy, so I figured it was only appropriate that I would get an off-the-wall kind of word. Now I had a good excuse to go fishing anyway.

Months passed and I began to forget what Howard had said.

Las Hadas

The company I worked for at the time had a huge sales perk and even though I wasn't in sales, they invited me along. Leanna and I got an all expense paid vacation to Las Hadas Mexico and away we went!

Las Hadas is a beautiful place down on the pacific coast of southern Mexico. The food was great and the accommodations were wonderful. It was a really neat thing for us to get to do. There was a day when we got to choose an excursion. We could either go scuba diving or deep sea fishing. Leanna wanted to go fishing, but I was afraid it would be like the last time I had gone deep sea fishing in the gulf; a 12 hour puke-fest.

Thank God she talked me into it. It was nothing like what I had thought it was going to be. There were six of us fishing on that boat and after a couple of hours, all six of us caught a sailfish at once! It was pure pandemonium! They only had one chair at the back and the rest of us had to just hang on the best we could, while one by one we began reeling them in. It took literally hours to bring those fish in. The boat captain told us that in all of his life, he had never caught six sailfish at one time.

After a long struggle, we were able to actually land 3 of the six we had hooked. When my line snapped, Leanna gladly handed me her pole. She had been hanging on for more than thirty minutes and she was about to let go. After another thirty minutes it was my turn in the chair and before long, I was up close with a nine-foot, six-inch sailfish! I had it stuffed and for more than ten years it hung on my living room wall.

I never will forget that night as I lay in bed exhausted. We were both almost asleep when Leanna calmly said, "Troy, do you remember the prophecy Howard gave you about catching a big fish?"

I nearly feel out of my bed.

The Message in the Miracle

The five fold ministry gifts that God has given to the church are listed in Eph 4:11-13. It says:

> *"And He Himself gave some to be apostles, some prophets, some evangelists, and some pastors and teachers, for the equipping of the saints for the work*

of ministry, for the edifying of the body of Christ, till
we all come to the unity of the faith and of the
knowledge of the Son of God, to a perfect man, to the
measure of the stature of the fullness of Christ;"
NKJV

The majority of Christians tend to validate the need for evangelists, pastors and teachers, while keeping the office of apostle and prophet in the "just-a-little-too-weird category". That's not necessarily a good move.

While these offices should be held accountable, they should not be dismissed because they are out of the norm. I think this miracle proves that what we need sometimes is an off-the-wall move of God. Something outside of our normal boundaries. Something that upsets the applecart of our understanding. Something that makes an impact! Something that is real and powerful and not prefabricated and normal.

I came back from Mexico knowing that God had a world wide ministry for me and it would not have happened had it not been for this miracle. I pray that God will touch you in an off-the-wall kind of way. Let yourself be vulnerable and let God do a different kind of work in your life!

I double-dog-dare you to sincerely ask God to touch you in an off-the-wall kind of way. I guarantee you, He has something in mind.

Chapter
9

**Something Better
Than Miracles**

Before you finish reading this book, I want to hit a homerun revelation into your part of the ballpark. If you've got your glove on, you could walk away from this book with a new bullet for your arsenal and a new strategy for your spiritual game plan.

There is a balance that needs to be taught concerning miracles. As much as I love miracles, I understand that most of the time a miracle is a short-term solution to a long-term malfunction. Miracles only happen in the most desperate of times and places. If you are somebody that needs a miracle, I certainly believe that God has one for you. The whole point of this book is to help you reach for the miracle you need. The balance to that is, I also believe that there is a better and more long-term way that God wants you to prosper.

First of all, let me tell you that miracles, as powerful as they are, are not God's best and God's highest way of prospering His people. The children of Israel wandered in the desert for forty years and prospered by a miracle every day they were out there, but as soon as they came into the Promised Land, the manna from heaven ceased to fall. Why is that you think?

Were they worse off in the Promised Land? No they weren't, they were finally in a better place. Then why did the miracle of provision stop once they crossed the Jordan? The answer is that the second their feet touched the muddy bottom of that river, they entered into a whole new set of rules for how God's people should prosper.

A Better Way to Prosper

There are 2 main ways that the Lord prospers His people. The first way is through **MIRACLES OF PROVISION**, but the better way is through a principle called **SEED- TIME & HARVEST**.

Seed-time and harvest is a real fancy term for a principle that illustrates work and reward. It's when you want something, so there becomes a certain work to produce the thing desired. This is a spiritual and a natural principle. Let me lay the whole thing out for you.

Number one, GOD WANTS YOU TO PROSPER! If you are ever confused as to what God's will is for your life, then find out what God's word is for your life. You can't separate His will and His word. They are one in the same. Here's the Word:

> *Beloved, I wish above all things that thou mayest*
> *prosper and be in health,*
> *even as thy soul prospereth.*
> *1 John 1:2*

It is God's will for you to prosper. He truly is in your corner. If God has a refrigerator, your picture is all over it! He's crazy about you and wants good things for you. But if you're going to tap into God's prosperity, you're going to have to take advantage of the way He wants to prosper you. You can wait for a miracle, but let me show you the problem with that.

As I have already stated, anytime you see God doing a miracle, you see somebody in a mess. As soon as they are out of that mess, the miracle stops and then the principle of seed-time and harvest kicks in. If they do not abide by that principle, they end up back in the mess that they were in before, hoping and believing for another miracle. Let's look at three famous biblical miracles of provision.

Jesus Feeding the Five-Thousand

And when the day began to wear away,
then came the twelve, and said unto him,
send the multitude away, that they may go into the
towns and country round about,
and lodge, and get victuals:
for we are here in a desert place.
Luke 9:12

Here's a famous miracle that I would have loved to have seen. The food just kept on coming! Basket after basket of the biggest buffet anybody had ever stood in line for appeared virtually out of thin air! The excitement must have been incredible and the feast must have been full of praise and just jaw-dropping wonder. I can just see Jesus laughing in delight as thousands began to pig-out on a feast that they had not expected. It really must have been something.

See the message in the miracle. The miracle only happened when it was a life or death situation. The Bible says they were in a desert place and there was no food there at all. In fact, the food that they desperately needed was in the towns, away from the place where they were at. The miracle of provision ended as soon as everybody got back to those towns and then there was a whole new set of rules to prosper with God.

Elijah and the Widow Woman

> *For thus saith the LORD God of Israel,*
> *the barrel of meal shall not waste,*
> *neither shall the cruse of oil fail,*
> *until the day that the LORD*
> *sendeth rain upon the earth.*
> *1 Kings 17:14*

Because of an incredible miracle, this woman made a mint when everybody was going through a national depression. If anybody needed oil or meal, they came to her and though she only had a small cruse, she poured out thousands of gallons of oil from it, through several years of famine. We all know the story and how that came to pass, but see the message in the miracle. So long as they were in a do or die situation, a famine to be precise, then the miracle took place, but the day it rained, God no longer prospered her by miracles. He prospered her another way.

The Israelites Get Fed Manna From Heaven

And the children of Israel did eat manna forty years,
until they came to a land inhabited;
they did eat manna,
until they came unto the borders
of the land of Canaan.
Exodus 16:35

We have already talked about this a little bit. Every morning for forty years they would wake up and find something on the ground that they never were able to identify. The Hebrew term for "what is it?" is manna. So they literally were eating something they couldn't figure out. They had what-is-it burgers, what-is-it casseroles, what-is-it on rye, what-is-it and gravy. Manna was a forty-year miracle that prospered God's people in a day they could not have prospered without it. The message in the miracle is found in the verse above. Once they crossed the borders of Canaan, what-is-it became a memory.

If miracle provision is God's best way of prospering us,
then the people of God really messed up when they
entered into the Promised Land!

No, miracles are God's way of helping us in very desperate times. If you are somebody that is going to live from miracle to miracle, then you are somebody that will constantly live in a famine. If the only way God can prosper you is through miracles, then your life is constantly in peril and on the edge of destruction. God has something better for you than that! He is willing to give you a miracle, but He is tired of you living in a famine.

Seed-time and Harvest: Work and Reward

Though it's not as instantaneous, it's just as miraculous
and it is much, much better. God wants to give you a
vision for something better, give you a plan to achieve
that better thing and then give you the ability to
maintain the thing He gives you.

God has designed His people so that we are at our
happiest when we are setting goals and achieving those
goals. Our lives are fulfilled by having a vision for
something better, finding a way to make that happen
and then finally living in that place. That's your
promised land and it's a lot better place to live, than
from miracle to miracle.

Like the fruit your kids don't eat in the kitchen, your
life if left alone, will begin to decay.
Sometimes we tend to sit on our blessed assurance,
while God's desire is for us to move into something
much better. Without a vision, you really will perish.
God wants you to do something with your life! He
wants you constantly headed into something better.

The Power of Momentum

Here is a great revelation for you to catch. God is revealed through many progressive steps and His will for
your life is also revealed in progressive steps. There is
a certain momentum that builds up when you begin to
achieve God-given goals and that momentum becomes
an impelling force of strength that enables you to land
in a better spot than you were before!

We have all seen the wonder of momentum. The natural principle that says, once something big gets started, it's really hard to stop. I witnessed a crashed Cuban airliner that went off the edge of the runway in Guatemala City, Guatemala. It was big. I think it was a 747. The wreckage is still there and I expect it will be for years because I noticed families had taken up residence in it.

When I got back to the states, I did some research on the airport in an attempt to find out what had happened. From various reports, it seems the fatal crash is a simple story of momentum. The pilot had never landed on the short runway before and he landed much later than he should have had. At the end of the runway is a cliff that drops off into the slums below. That poor pilot desperately tried to stop his aircraft as he slammed on the breaks and reversed his thrusters, but because of the momentum of that huge jet airliner, he ran out of runway and went over the cliff. At the end of that runway, as we were taking off, I could see grooves in the pavement that went straight off into nothing. Awesome is the power of momentum.

The Bible clearly states that our relationship with God is one of constant forward progression. That's why we tend to call it a "walk" with God. It's one that starts off small on our part, but the longer we walk with God, the bigger steps He requires of us and enables us to take.

In Isaiah 28:13 we move from line to line and from precept to precept. It also says we move forward here a little and there a little.

In Romans 1:17 we move from faith to faith.
In 2 Corinthians 3:18 we move from glory to glory.

> In Psalms 41:13 we move from
> everlasting unto everlasting.
> In Psalms 42:7 we move from deep to deep.

The whole point is that we move from point-to-point. No matter where you are at, God always has a better point for you to go to within your reach! There is an impelling force of strength involved with forward progression. Once you meet a God given goal, you have a new ability to meet another goal.

NEVER UNDERESTIMATE THE POWER OF MOMENTUM. If God can do one thing in your life, then He can do two. If God can do two things in your life, then He can do four. If God can give you the wisdom, favor and character to get a raise at your work, then He can do the same thing to give you a higher position in your work. If He can give you a higher position, then He can give you a plan to achieve a better job altogether. Once you are living by God given plans and dreams, you are truly living by faith. It's not just a Sunday thing.

I would much rather walk with God in a house paid-off and free of debt, than prosper by a miracle in the midst of seeing my house repossessed and sold to somebody else. I would much rather live with the Lord day-to-day in a good state of health, than prosper by miraculously living with a terrible disease. If there is any way I can avoid that disease, then it is better to be led into a different place by the power of God.

Better to Not Need a Miracle

I have a good friend that has made millions in the cable TV business. He has seen the Lord prosper him abun-

dantly in a better way, than through miracles. He sees
certain things that he wants to achieve, he finds a way
to make it happen and he maintains it though hard work
and creative handling.

This is a step-by-step process that requires the hand of
the Lord on a day-to-day basis. My brother Todd and
my brother-in-law Daniel both decided that they didn't
want to be poor all their lives when they were very
young. So they went to college and learned how to
work on airplanes. Today they are both in management
for a huge company and they don't need a financial
miracle.

This is not just a hard work principle. Hard work is a
big part of it, but if all you needed was hard work to
prosper, then every coal miner in West Virginia would
be a billionaire. Here's what the better way to prosper
looks like.

(1) God gives you a vision for something better.
(2) God gives you a specific plan to make that happen.
(3) God hooks you up with the right people and the
    right tools.
(4) God gives you the guts and the courage to pull it off
    and maintain it.
(5) God prospers you and people shake their heads and
    wonder how come you're blessed.

Now that's a lot better than needing a miracle!

If you're going to prosper this way with God, then there
are at least three things you're going to have to be de-
pendant on God for. Instead of a quick fix miracle,
you're going to need the gifts of **wisdom, favor and**

character. These three triplets are the tools that God gives His people that want to long-term prosper.

> *And Jesus increased in wisdom and stature,*
> *and in favour with God and man.*
> *Luke 2:52*

Let's look at them one at a time.

WISDOM

Wisdom is the God given ability to see and know things that are not obvious to others. Wisdom is the ability to think beyond your circumstances and even your own training. Wisdom is vision for something greater and the understanding of how to make that happen. Wisdom is a free download from God.

> *If any of you lack wisdom, let him ask of God,*
> *that giveth to all men liberally,*
> *and upbraideth not; and it shall be given him.*
> *James 1:5*

Wisdom is knowing when to move and how to move. Wisdom is being led by the Lord to apply for a better job at a certain time, even though it is way out of your league. Wisdom can be a Spirit led investment at a critical time. I don't know if you have seen a picture of what the first team of Microsoft looked like. They look more like a bunch of gypsies and hippies, rather than the richest and most powerful people in the world. Had you invested in them in that day, it would have been wisdom and you would not be needing a financial miracle right now.

There are other trains out there that are steaming into better places. You just need the wisdom to know which one to climb on board with. Read James 1:5 again and see if it is God's will for you to have wisdom.

FAVOR

Favor is the God given ability to hook up with the right people to prosper. Favor is when God causes people to support you and back you up. Favor is when people like you and they don't really even know why. Favor is what you need on a job interview. Favor is what you need when it's times for a promotion. Favor is what you need when you go to the bank with your vision for a new business. Favor is what you need to be the top sales person. Favor is what God gives you to beat the odds against you.

> *Let them shout for joy, and be glad,*
> *that favour my righteous cause:*
> *yea, let them say continually,*
> *let the LORD be magnified,*
> *which hath pleasure in the*
> *prosperity of His servant.*
> *Psalms 35:27*

Favor goes hand-in-hand with character. God gave Joseph favor when he was in his master's house and when he was in prison. God gave Joseph favor even with the Pharaoh himself. But Joseph knew how to be the perfect house slave, how to be the model prisoner and how to conduct himself around a king. Not only did he have the wisdom to know these things, he had the character to do those things when it was not easy to do it. He was somebody that God could prosper.

CHARACTER

It does no good to know how to get your dream job, and to have favor with your boss so that you get hired for your dream job, if you don't have the character to get up and go to work when you do not feel like it. Character is the God given ability to make the right choice when most would not. Character is working harder than you ever have for your goals, even when you don't see an immediate payoff. Character is going to work when most would stay home, doing the job when most would shut down and pressing forward when most would give up. Character is constantly making something happen.

He becometh poor that dealeth with a slack hand: but the hand of the diligent maketh rich.
Proverbs 10:4

Wealth gotten by vanity shall be diminished: but he that gathereth by labour shall increase.
Proverbs 13:11

Joseph, whom I have already been talking about, is the perfect model of how God wants to ultimately bless all of us. When a miracle was required, he believed God and got that miracle, but the main way he prospered was through being the best at serving. God gave him a vision, then he gave him the ability to get to that place of vision through wisdom, favor and character.

He knew a secret that a lot of folks don't. When he was serving his master, he didn't see it as serving his master, he saw it as serving the Lord. When he was in prison, he saw it serving the Lord, when he was in

Pharaoh's court, his perception was the same. See, his attitude was that no one could keep him from serving the Lord, no matter what task was put in front of him; therefore he prospered at every task put in front of him. Nearly 2,000 years later, Paul recognized this same principle when he penned down his book that we would call Colossians.

Servants, obey in all things your masters according to the flesh; not with eyeservice, as menpleasers; but in singleness of heart, fearing God: And whatsoever ye do, do it heartily, as to the Lord, and not unto men; Knowing that of the Lord ye shall receive the reward of the inheritance: for ye serve the Lord Christ.
Colossians 3:22-24

If you want to quit being in a situation that requires a miracle when it comes to finances, I encourage you to have the attitude that nobody can keep you from serving God. Serve God whether you're flipping a hamburger or writing a ticket on the side of the highway. Serve God whether you are cleaning apartments or preaching a funeral. Whatever you do, do it with all your heart, as unto the Lord and watch your life move into a better promise.

Miracles are wonderful, but they are not God's best way to prosper you. Having the Lord involved into every area of your life and being led by His Spirit into God given goals is far better than desperately living by miracles. Praise God that He always has something better.

Right now might be a great time to pray and ask the Lord to increase your vision. Ask God to enlarge your heart. Ask God to give you His heart's desires for your life. Tell Him you're tired of living in the same old mess and ask the Lord to give you a straight path out. Some God given goals and some God given plans to reach those goals are what you need to change your financial situation on a long-term basis and that is something better than a miracle.

Thou wilt show me the path of life:
in thy presence is fullness of joy;
at thy right hand there
are pleasures for evermore.
Psalms 16:11

Chapter 10

A Final Miracle

There have been lots of other major and minor miracles that I am privy to. A friend of mine was burned horribly in a terrible fire and miraculously the Lord saved him in every way a man can be saved. The boss of my brother was completely healed of Hepatitis C. Back in 1986, God healed my leg from what we Texans call a "fiddle-back" spider bite, preventing me from having surgery and serving as a powerful witness to the people I worked with. These are the kinds of things miracle believers see happen these days. These are the kinds of things God is doing for His people in every hour, on every continent. As I have already told you, these are the days.

My cousin nearly drowned while surfing off the northern coast of California and under the water he had a special visitation of the Lord. My brother and my brother-in-law were both miraculously saved when the landing gear of the C-130 aircraft they were both working on failed. There are lots of other stories to tell and many other messages within those miracles, but to keep this book from being an encyclopedia, we will have to visit those miracles another time.

All of these miracles are common, and for the most part unknown, but there are at least 36 miracles that have been famous for two thousand years. The miracles of Jesus proved to the world that there is a God that can change anything for the betterment of His people and for the glory of the Father. With some help from The Boston Christian Bible Study Resources, (**www.bcbsr.com**) let's take a look at the miracles of Jesus and what Gospel records them.

Nature Miracles	Matt	Mark	Luke	John
1. Stilling the Storm	8:23	4:35	8:22	_
2. Feeding the 5000	14:13	6:30	9:10	6:1
3. Walking on the Water	14:25	6:48	_	6:19
4. Feeding the 4000	15:32	8:1	_	_
5. Temple Tax in the Fish's Mouth	17:24	_	_	_
6. Withering the Fig Tree	21:18	11:12	_	_
7. Draught of Fish	_	_	5:1	_
8. Turning Water into Wine	_	_	_	2:1
9. Second Draught of Fish	_	_	_	21:1

Healing Miracles	Matt	Mark	Luke	John
General Healings				
1. Cleansing of a Leper	8:2	1:40	5:12	_
2. Healing a Centurion's Servant	8:5	_	7:1	_
3. Healing Peter's Mother-in-law	8:14	1:30	4:38	_
4. Healing the Sick at evening	8:16	1:32	4:40	_
5. Healing a paralytic	9:2	2:3	5:18	_
6. Healing the Hemorrhaging woman	9:20	5:25	8:43	_
7. Healing Two Blind Men	9:27	_	_	_
8. Healing a Man's Withered Hand	12:9	3:1	6:6	_
9. Healing the Gentile Woman's Daughter	15:21	7:24	_	_
10. Healing the Epileptic Boy	17:14	9:17	9:38	_
11. Healing a Blind Men	20:30	10:46	18:35	_
12. Healing a Deaf Mute	_	7:31	_	_
13. Healing a Blind Man at Bethsaida	_	8:22	_	_
14. Healing the Infirm, Bent Woman	_	_	13:11	_
15. Healing the Man with Dropsy	_	_	14:1	_
16. Cleansing the Ten Lepers	_	_	17:11	_
17. Restoring a Servant's Ear	_	_	22:51	_
18. Healing the Nobleman's Son (of fever)	_	_	_	4:46
19. Healing an Infirm Man at Bethesda	_	_	_	5:1
20. Healing the Man born blind 8:2	_	_	_	9:1

Resurrections	Matt	Mark	Luke	John
1. Raising the Ruler's Daughter	9:18,23	5:22,35	8:40,49	_
2. Raising of a Widow's Son at Nain	_	_	7:11	_
3. Raising of Lazarus	_	_	_	11:43
Casting out Demons				
1. Demons entering a herd of swine	8:28	5:1	8:26	_
2. Curing a Demon-possessed Mute	9:32	_	_	_
3. Casting Out an Unclean Spirit	_	1:32	4:33	_
4. Curing a Demon-possessed, Blind and Mute man	12:22	_	11:14	_

We learn so much about Jesus when we look at the miracles He did. When the Holy Spirit moves upon the images that are bouncing off of the back of our eyes as we read these biblical accounts, we walk away with conclusions like:

What is the storm compared to the God that walks on it?
(Jesus walks on the water)
What looks like absolute finality is merely a short nap when Jesus shows up.
(Raising the ruler's daughter)
There is no limit to how God can bless me or what he can use to do it!
(The coin in the fish's mouth)

God loves people that others are scared of.
(Curing of a demon possessed man)
God understands the importance
of special times in our lives.
(The water turned into wine at the wedding)
God hates false advertisement.
(Jesus cursed the fig tree)

There's a message in every miracle, to every hearer, at every level of faith. God loves to get His point across. If he can do it through a miracle, He has proved at least in these 36 times, that He is willing to do it.

The Most Important Miracle

Out of all the miracles that God has ever done through anyone throughout the centuries, there is one miracle that all miracles hinge upon. When you get the message in this one miracle, it changes how you see things and even who you are.

This miracle has to be real or all of Christianity is not real. This miracle is the deciding factor and the simplest litmus test in proving if the deity and the gospel of Jesus Christ is fact or fantasy, truth or fable.

This one miracle separates Jesus from every man ever born.

This miracle is despised by the critics and reviled in the demonic realm more than any other.

It's the miracle we celebrate every Easter; the Resurrection of Jesus Christ.

The Heart Of Christianity

The Resurrection of Jesus Christ is the very heart of all Christianity. In 1 Corinthians 15, the renowned troublemaker known as Paul, wrote and reasoned, "If Christ has not been raised, our preaching is useless and so is your faith". This is something that has to be real. Paul, being as subtle as a meat cleaver, continued to spell it out when he said, "If Christ has not been raised, your faith is futile; you are still in your sins. Then those also who have fallen sleep in Christ are lost. If only for this life we have hope in Christ, we are to be pitied more than all men." But then Paul triumphantly declared, "But Christ has indeed been raised from the dead, the firstfruits of those who have fallen asleep".

See, the most important miracle has the most important message. If this miracle really happened, then it says that Jesus Christ has truly slapped death in the face and that makes His credentials as God almighty irrefutable. No wonder people don't want to believe in the Resurrection! If He did indeed raise himself from the dead, then He is indeed who He says He is and even more; if He is who He says He is, then that means the critics are who He says they are and people have a problem with that!

Why Should I Believe in the Resurrection?

For one thing, you don't have to believe everything. God does not require you to buy into everything that a preacher says. If you don't believe the true stories I have typed out in this book, you have not lost very much, but if you don't believe in the Resurrection of Jesus Christ you have lost everything. Without the message of this miracle taking up residence in your heart, everything in your life is like furniture in a house that will burn to the ground. You best not fall in love with it.

If there is a Johnny Cochren like "spirit" within you that causes you to doubt what is so obvious to so many millions, I've got good news for you. Faith does not require you to check your brain at the door. The belief in the Resurrection of Christ is a reasonable faith that has been thought through and found out by the world's most brilliant people. People like Sir Isaac Newton, who was smart enough to change the face of science. People like the founding fathers of our nation, that were smart enough to change the face of the world.

Before you decide that you are smarter than the billions of lives that have been changed by this one miracle, let me give you some reasonable reasons why I believe you should buy into it.

Verifiable Proof

If you wanted to verify the miracles I am reporting here, it wouldn't be that hard. For instance, since I am writing this book in a day when those I am writing about are still living, all you would have to do is ask of them if this was true. You could directly go to these people I am writing about and just ask them.

As an example, if you wanted to find out if my brother's boss was really completely healed of hepatitis C, then all you would have to do is find out who my brother is and call him. If you did not believe him, you could ask him who his boss is and then go ask his boss if he was really healed of a non-curable disease and was it accurate that I reported it as hepatitis C. When he confirmed all of it was true, you still might decide that there is some kind of conspiracy between the 3 of us, because you are too smart to believe in miracles, so you could go to his family and to his doctors to find out if indeed he had nearly died of this terrible disease and if indeed he was completely cured without any traces left of it in his body. Once the doctors showed you the diagnosis before and after the miracle, you could believe that they were mistaken in their diagnosis and then go back to your original belief that you are smarter than the people who believe in miracles, which is why nothing could convince you in the first place.

The point I am making is that, because I am writing this in the day the people involved with these miracles are still alive, you don't have to be a dummy to believe what I am saying, because it is all easily verifiable. Likewise, the time that the New Testament was written and the Resurrection story told, was a day when it could all be verified. The people involved were still alive when the writers wrote about them, and all you had to do was go and ask them. The fact is that, when their names were mentioned in connection with Jesus Christ, they were immediately put on a hit list, and if it weren't true, they would have come forward. Besides that, if you didn't believe them, all you had to do was go and ask the people that knew them and they would tell you the difference in the person's life from before he or she saw Jesus resurrected, to after their sighting.

If it was all a hoax, then the fast moving bullet of Christianity would have hit the ground like a dud when the stories became printed and people began to come forward saying that what had been written about them was just not true.

Another thing to consider is, that Jesus didn't just show up at one time, to one or two people. He walked and talked with hundreds and hundreds for a full forty days before His ascension.

Check this out, the Bible, in a day when these people were still alive to verify it, says that Jesus appeared to all of the following people. Another thing to consider is that these were not just fleeting glimpses of spooky apparitions. These were times when Jesus sat down with them to eat, gave them great big bear hugs, taught them the scriptures and walked with them from one place to another. These were not just sightings; these people said that for forty days they literally "hung out" with Jesus, just as they had before He went to the cross. Here are those that met with Jesus after His Resurrection:

Mary Magdalene in the garden in John 20
To the other girls on the same day in Matthew 22
To Cleopas and another guy on the road
to a town called Emmaus Luke 24
To a whole room full of people in Luke 24
To the ten apostles when
Thomas wasn't there in John 20
To Thomas and the other apostles in John 20
To all eleven disciples
on the mountain in Matthew 28:16

**To the apostles and other folks on
the Mount of Olives in Luke 24 and Acts 1
At least 500 other people
that Paul knew of in 1 Corinthians 15:11**

So you see, if you had lived 2,000 years ago when the
book was first written, you could have gone to any one
of these hundreds of people and verified if the
Resurrection was the truth. Had you gone to Peter, he
would have convinced you by saying exactly what he
wrote in his 2nd letter.

*For we have not followed cunningly devised fables,
when we made known unto you
the power and coming of our Lord Jesus Christ,
but were eyewitnesses of His majesty.
2 Peter 1:16*

Ok, now that you have gone to Peter and asked him,
"Why should you believe him or any other disciple for
that matter?"…let's talk about that.

The Dirty Dozen

Those twelve people that Jesus picked up and chose to
carry His gospel, were men of no notoriety before Jesus
recruited them. They were all different ages, from different walks of life. They didn't really prove
themselves before they walked with Jesus or really
even while they walked with Jesus. They were only together in the ministry of Christ for 3 1/2 years. After
Jesus was crucified, these guys did the only thing they
could do. First they hid for a couple of days until
things died down, then they went back home and back

to their jobs, disgraced and feeling like the biggest failures in the world.

Peter said, "I'm going fishing", this of course after he had proved he could curse like the sailor he was when Jesus was being tortured at the temple.

Thomas had decided he had tried the Jesus thing and it just wasn't for him anymore, telling John that unless he could thrust his hand up in the wound of His side he wanted nothing to do with Jesus. It was this same Thomas that Jesus walked up to, lifting up his shirt and saying, "Go ahead Thomas, do what you've got to do to believe that it is I". I tell you that I really believe Jesus came to each one of these guys just as they said, and this is why.

These were the guys that ran like a bunch of scared rabbits when Jesus was arrested. These are the guys that denied even knowing him. All of them except for John didn't even show up at the cross for fear of being recognized. Yet, this same exact group of guys, minus Judas Iscariot, is the same guys that are turning the world upside down just a month later. Just one month later everything changed. On the day of Pentecost, the same Peter that had been too scared to let people know that he was associated with Jesus, stood up and preached at a street outreach in downtown Jerusalem in broad daylight! He was so convincing that 3,000 people were saved in one day!

All 11 of these men went throughout the whole world. There was nothing you could do to stop them or to shut them up. Do you know what they were saying?

**HE'S ALIVE!   HE'S RESURRECTED!!!
HE'S NOT JUST A MAN, HE'S GOD!
WE SAW HIM!   WE ATE WITH HIM!
WE SAW HIM ASCEND INTO HEAVEN!**

These same men that had been so fearful of death, no longer feared it at all. Every one of them, not just *some*, but *all* of them, stuck to their story even though it cost them everything. Every one of them continued telling the same story even as they were being executed thousands of miles apart from each other, and years into the future.

"He's alive!", they would say. "We saw Him!", they would say.

Not only did they not change their stories when they were being killed, but they did not change their story as their families were being killed. Death did not have the sting it once had and the grave no longer had victory over them. They had understood the message in the miracle of the Resurrection.

These guys didn't retire to posh estates after many years of preaching at conventions and autographing Bibles. Church history records the penalty these men paid for preaching the message of the ultimate miracle.

James was beheaded by Herod in Jerusalem.

Peter went to Asia Minor, the British Isles, and Spain. He was crucified in Rome, upside down.

Andrew (Peter's brother) went to Greece and southern Russia. He was also crucified on an X shaped cross known as Andrew's cross.

Philip went to Gaul (which is modern France) where stoned, drawn and quartered and then his remains were hung up in Hierapolis.

Bartholomew went to Armenia and was flayed or skinned alive.

Thomas went to Persia and India. He was killed with a spear, while he was preaching in India.

Matthew went to Ethiopia and was attacked and killed by sword, while visiting Egypt.

James the lesser, preached right there in Palestine and later went to Egypt, where it is thought he was crucified.

Jude preached in Assyria and in Persia. He was killed in Persia.

Simon the Canaanite went to Egypt, to Africa and later Britain and was crucified.

Mathias, the apostle that took the place of Judas, was stoned and then beheaded in Jerusalem.

John lived to very old, having survived torture, including being boiled in oil. He spent his latter years a prisoner on the island of Patmos and died a free man in Ephesus nearly 70 years after the Resurrection of Christ.

Had any of these men not seen Jesus resurrected, they would have said so. The Jews and the Gentiles that hated Christianity were chomping at the bits to find some inconsistency or ultimately a denial of them having seen Jesus alive after He had been crucified. When they couldn't find it, they just snuffed them out and not a one of them changed their tune!

They didn't, simply because the Resurrection was an undeniable fact to them. As I have already said, death no longer had it's sting. The threat of death doesn't have very much weight to a man that personally knows Jesus has slapped it in the face for all of us.

If you cant believe the resurrection after contemplating that, may be this will help you. The Picture of me on the back of this book was taken at the garden Tomb in Jerusalem Israel. You can take my word for it. I have been to his grave and he is not there!

The Message in Every Miracle

You can say what you want about miracles. You can scoff at the notion that God intervenes in the lives of desperate people. You can reason away every good thing that God has ever done. You can hang on to pride and think that the rest of us are stupid, but know this for certain, the words you are reading now are there because a nineteen year old boy cried out to Jesus many years ago.

He is the kind of God that wants to keep you from stepping onto a plane that's going to crash. He is the kind of God that is willing to replace your ratty roof with a brand new one. He is so sympathetic and wonderful, that He knows how to make blind eyes see and even seeing eyes blind, if that's what it is you need.

If you do not know Him, all you have to do is genuinely seek Him and cry out to Him. He will make Himself known to you and in that day, you will know the greatest of all miracles. Resurrected life will come to live in you. Miracles are real because Jesus is real. Miracles are amazing because Jesus is amazing.

That's the message I get when I see a miracle.

About the Author

Troy Brewer is founder and Senior Pastor of Open Door Ministries Church near Joshua Texas. His Food Outreach Ministry gives away hundreds of thousands of pounds of food every year to the poor of north Texas. This has proved to be fertile ground for amazing moves of the Lord.

His missionary journeys have taken him to the jungles of Uganda, Costa Rica, and to the Middle East. He regularly preaches to congregations in Central America, Mexico and in London, England. This collection of miracles is a result of those contacts.

A versatile man of God, his singing and songwriting has received airplay literally all over the world and at this time he has five praise albums to his credit.

He resides in Johnson county Texas with his wife Leanna and his four children, Maegan, Benjamin, Luke and Rhema. This is his first book.

Always busy and always available to preach, he can be contacted at Po Box 1349 Joshua TX 76058 or by phone: 1-817-297-6911.

www.opendoorministries.org www.troybrewer.org

If this book has been a blessing to you, please write us or sign our guest book on our website

"Don't just look for a miracle, look for the miracle worker, Jesus."

Pastor Troy at the garden tomb in Jerusalem, 2002.

CPSIA information can be obtained
at www.ICGtesting.com
Printed in the USA
FSOW01n1229241214
4135FS